Essays

of

Contemporary Conscience

"A new look at old ideas"

Cover Design: Roopnarain Persaud

Publisher: RDS Multiservices

Copyright by Roopnarain Persaud © 2017

Contact: 646 Deauville Court, Kissimmee, FL 34758.

ISBN – 10: 1 9 7 6 2 7 2 7 6 9

ISBN - 13: 9 7 8 1 9 7 6 2 7 2 7 6 9

Essays

Of

Contemporary Conscience

(2017)

By

Aurora Spring

Dedicated to

Amendment 1 of the Constitution of the United States of America

TABLE of CONTENTS

Essay #1 "Licensed for Fraud"...Page 5

Essay (Poem) #2 "Harvesting of Souls" ....Page 12

Essay # 3 "The 225th Bill of Rights (USA)
Anniversary"..Page 14

Essay #4 "The Conservation of Matter" ....Page 29

Essay #5 "Is the New God "Democracy?"......................Page 33

Essay #6 "Wars: Why We Have Them?"........................Page 39

Essay #7 "Who Speaks for Americans; Who Secures the Financial
Interest of Americans?"..Page 59

Essay #8 "Peace and Conflict"....................................Page 64

Essay #9 "To Believe or To Know"............................Page 99

Essay #10 "How Equal Are We?"...............................Page 107

Essay # 11 "Failure by Design"..................................Page 113

Essay #12 "Mr. & Ms. US Citizen"............................Page 120

Essay #13 "Indentureship"..Page 145

Essay #14 "For Feeling...Page 155

Essay #15 "The Guyana Situation".............................Page 162

(168 Pages)

"Licensed for Fraud"

The young boy was very hungry. He attempted to pick up a croissant that was on the counter at the deli. The owner of the deli grabbed his hand while he was still clutching the pastry and ordered the staff to call the local police. The police arrived, handcuffed the child and took him to the police station where he was ridiculed, verbally abused about his behavior, and accused that his behavior is typical of his race. He was tried and found guilty and was sentenced. He was branded with a "record" from an early age. As cattle was used to be branded, with skin-scars etched deep into their hides that remained noticeable for many years, so the child was branded with a police record, which will be brought up in court again and again for the rest of his life. The owner of the deli was vindicated and perhaps bragged, "how I caught one of them." The police gained credit towards his promotion.

The fellow, in his forties, was well dressed according to western fashion and style: you know, Armani suit, expensive tie, Maui Jim sunglasses and shining leather

Italian shoes. He appeared to be at the top of his game. He had a brisk and purposeful gait as he entered the skyscraper on Wall Street. He is what we call a "wall street banker."

The "wall street banker" spent a month or so designing a mortgage product, which we have come to call the "subprime" loan. He was happy with himself. The mortgage product will do the job. What is the job? We will see.

Folks, pursuing "the American Dream," wish to purchase houses to be transformed into their homes. They apply for mortgages through mortgage brokers. The Wall Street banks will pay the mortgage brokers when the real estate deals are closed. The Wall Street bankers will sell the mortgages on Wall Street. They will sell them to European and other banks and private investors.

The Wall Street banks and the mortgage brokers stated in writing that borrowers qualified for the loans and subsequently issued a written commitment to the borrowers. The commitment to lend the money was issued after the senior experts analyzed the variety of loan documents, which *they prescribed* that they need to make their decision to make the loans to finance the sale/purchase. They earn six-figure salaries and sachet about town with high-maintenance blonds and brunettes and mini-skirted "babes:" ***"life is good!"***

Oops! Millions of homeowners cannot afford to pay their mortgages, especially the subprime mortgages. Their houses are going into foreclosure. The Wall Street bankers made millions in points and fees from the borrowers whom **they said** qualified for the loans, which the banks financed. The Wall Street bankers made more millions from the sale of the subprime loans to European banks and others! The mortgage servicing departments made millions from servicing the mortgages. But now the homeowners cannot make their monthly mortgage payments and the house of cards come crashing down; the mortgage bauble bursts; the grand design is a great success for the banking few and America is placed in a recession. European banks and other investors are in serious financial trouble. The world's major economies are in crisis mode.

Millions of Americans lose their homes, lost their savings, and are effectively kicked onto the pavement. But the Wall Street bankers are not handcuffed, and are not placed in jail and do not get branded with a police record for the rest of their lives. They are at liberty to open a new corporation to start a new "business" to make more millions. They have access to Money! They can buy justice…you know…… *everything is for sale in America!*

The Government – the said Government that licensed them and the said Government that was supposed to monitor them, has since taken some of the banks to Court. Why did the Government's monitors not recognize the fraud (sophisticated theft) sooner? In fact not only did the Government not recognize the theft and call it theft, the Government declared that the banks "are too big to fail." The Government "bailed" them out by lending them taxpayers' money.

The banks have since paid back the loans with interest. The Government made money from the disaster designed and executed by the banks – from the engineered recession!

Well, the Government can lend money to the banks because the Government gets free money from taxpayers. The Government takes money from the paychecks of American workers right off the top, even before the workers themselves get any. The Government uses these trillions of dollars throughout the year without having to pay interest to taxpayers. When the Government borrows money from the banks, however, the banks charge interest. The Government uses taxpayers' money to pay the interests and principal to the banks. The Government is a conduit for workers' money upward and into the banks, especially the Federal Reserve Bank, a private institution.

Why the Government did not assist the homebuyers who suffered personal financial and emotional losses. You know, money equals life: when one loses one's money, one is losing all those years it took her/him to save that money that she/he invested to purchase that property. When the property is foreclosed, the best portion of her/his life goes to waste, never to be regained. Those who stole her/his money are like cannibals, eating the blood and body of those whose money they engineered to steal. Capitalism, when practiced as we have seen, becomes another word for cannibalism.

Let's talk about what happens in the Courts. Some of the banks are found "guilty" and are fined. The Government collects billions in fines from the banks but the bankers are not imprisoned. The banks are corporations. Corporations cannot be jailed or imprisoned – they are artificial persons!

Now, let's review. The kings and queens of England licensed the privateers to roam the high seas and they received a share of the plunder and the booty! Likewise the Government licensed the banks.

When the banks are found guilty of fraud in the Courts, the Government demands that the banks pay fines – demands some of the plunder or booty from the banks! Once the banks pay up, they can go on doing business.

Once the privateers paid up, they could have continued in their licensed profession – plunder, murder, and theft on the high seas, as citizens of England.

Have the homeowners called the police on the banks and mortgage brokers, like the owner of the deli? He called the police to lock up the child but, if his house was foreclosed, did he call the police on the bank? The bank sold him a mortgage product that was most unsuitable for him but was most suitable for the bank – a "subprime" loan that the bank gambled with, hoping that he would have paid it. The banks made the mortgage loan for a term of thirty (30) years.

Who can guarantee that a homeowner will be continuously employed for a period of thirty (30) years? Every homeowner must find work in the Economy but no one homeowner has control of the Economy. So how can he/she expect to pay her/his monthly mortgage payments every successive month for thirty (30) years?

The Government, with its army of experts, its various policies, and its bungling tiers of bureaucrats has the responsibility of controlling the Economy. But, when the Economy goes into a recession, or is engineered into a recession, the individual homeowners are held responsible for the debt that the banks said they qualified for and could pay.

The Government declared that the banks are too big to fail and the Courts, with its decisions, declared that they are too rich to jail.

The said Government passed "Anti-trust" Laws, which said Laws were enacted to prevent "monopoly" and ensure "competition" in an "open market free enterprise" economy, and which said government approved the mammoth mergers to make them too big to fail. *What hypocrisy and licensed fraud!*

Essay (Poem) #2

HARVESTING of SOULS

As the lotus from the depth and dark doth grow

And flowers with a beauty only to be plucked to

Decorate the life and living room of a greedy damsel,

There to whither and eventually die and be discarded;

And then another flower that struggled and fought

Its way to blossom and bloom, briefly and free,

Is similarly plucked to be in a bouquet to enhance

The artfulness and glory, the décor and decorum and

"Enjoyed" by those who never lift a finger in its care, or even knew of its existence or struggles to beauty,

So too the queen plucks the few who, in spite of her

Oppression, suppression and control, rise to fame,

Harvesting their bodies, minds and souls in her case and cause and

And missions and purpose, which are always

The same: to oppress, to suppress, to control, to deny,

To prevent their very existence, to deny their growing

And blossoming. She now, in exchange for three letters – "s, i, r" -

Sir now somebodies willingly advance the missions and purpose, the oppression and propaganda of the

Queen who oppressed them, stifling their very selves,

Harvesting their bodies,
minds and souls.

At dinners and pageants
and with designs

Unknown to them as
they wither away

In spirit and soul, and,
like mold in the cold,

They die, one by one in
the attempt for "sir" and,

Like the lotus and other
flowers, are then
discarded in decay, their
souls having been
harvested by a queen
that oppressed them all!

THE 225th BILL OF RIGHTS (USA) ANNIVERSARY (Essay #3)

As I listened to the discussion on C-SPAN to mark/celebrate the 225th Anniversary of the Bill of Rights on Sunday April 16th 2017, the following thoughts became clear to me:

(a) The Judges are not clear as to what the words in the Bill of Rights do mean. (What the writers of the Bill of Rights meant with the words they used.)

(b) Different Judges interpret the same word(s) differently, and, thus, apply their personal different interpretations onto the case(s) before her/him, and, thus, guide the jury (when there is one in the case) to different conclusions. This means that a "guilty" or "innocent" ruling is subject to the adjudicating judge's personal interpretation of the Bill of Rights and NOT the Right(s) protected by and in the Bill of Rights. This poses the question: When someone speaks or writes, how does a listener or reader know the meaning of the word(s) used, and, how must the word(s) be interpreted. Why are the personal interpretations of judges applied to the question/issue, or person, being adjudicated, and not the law?

(c) Further, a more universal issue (in addition to the issues of meaning and interpretation of words) is the issue of judging and ruling in favor, or against, an individual who was never aware of her/his rights in the Bill of Rights. In other words she/he is being judged with "laws" of which she/he has no knowledge. This is just what the British did. They made laws, which said laws were used by them to "judge their subjects," without "their subjects" having any knowledge of the existence and meaning, or interpretation, of the said British made law(s). As the British said, "ignorance of the law is no excuse." The American Constitution attempted to do away with this intentional and widely practiced injustice because it is unjust to "judge" someone without that someone having knowledge of the law with which she/he is being judged. Perhaps, if she/he knew of the law(s), she/he might have complied with them.

(d) How can someone be required to be in full compliance with a law when she/he has never been taught the law(s)? If we are to ever achieve a "just" society, the state(s) and federal government of the USA must ensure that the basic tenets of the law(s), the Bill of Rights, are continuously taught at all levels of education. Since this is not currently happening, the American revolution, as a departure from the British monarchical control and abuse, is a farce and is far from achieving a fair and just society where law(s) are made by the people, for the people in a Democratic society. We have not put in place the mechanics (curricula in our schools) that is necessary to achieve a Democratic society in which the individual citizen is equipped with the basic civic knowledge of the Bill of Rights with which she/he is properly informed of her/his rights and so can participate properly, if not fully, in the touted democracy.

(e) The summation of the current system is that we the people must trust and have faith in the judges and what they do. Isn't this what religions ask us to do, to have faith and believe? What is the difference then between law and religion? To judge one must have evidence, not "faith" and "belief." And, any way, how can one have "faith" and "belief" in what judges do while being ignorant of the law(s) because the states made no provisions for the teaching of even the basic meanings and interpretations of the law(s) and, thus, the law(s) remain a mystery both to the public and the judges themselves? This is another reason why justice is a farce.

Justice is further dependent upon and is affected by: **(i)** the police; **(ii)** the witness; **(iii)** the ability of the lawyer chosen; **(iv)** the financial capacity of the accused.

The Police force is made up of individuals, each with her/his own personal prejudices: racial, religious, ethnic, egocentric, and gender. Each individual police officer has the opportunity to exercise personal discretion when deciding whether or not to take an action to bring an offending citizen (supposedly/allegedly) before the Courts: she/he decides whether, or not, according to her/his judgment, the citizen has engaged in an "offensive" act or behavior.

So, Police Officer Henry can apprehend citizen Malcolm for behavior "Y" while citizen John may not be apprehended by the same Police Officer for the same behavior "Y." And, another Police Officer may choose to "excuse" Malcolm but apprehend Henry for the same "Y" behavior – discretionary authority.

When the police apprehend someone, and bring her/him before the Courts, the Judges are more likely to give credence to the police's account of the incident and not the accused. What gives a police officer the exclusive right to the truth or facts of the incident being reported? As I have seen in so many Court cases on the TV (Judge Judy and others) the Judges state emphatically to defending or complaining citizens that "I do not believe you." So, here again, it is not the law(s) that operate, it is the Judge's belief. When the Judge does not believe the individual's story (her account of or his version of the case before the Judge) that individual will lose her/his case.   Can Justice be served in this manner?

The case against the accused is further biased against her/him by and with "witness(es)." The Police can and do bring manufactured "witness(es)" to testify in Court. The accused may also bring witness(es) to support her/his version of the incident. The Judges, however, are predisposed to believe the Police witness(es).   The Judges' beliefs, not law(s) – the Bill of Rights – reigns supreme and informs and affects the outcome of the case(s) before the Judge. Yes, there is the right to appeal. This costs money, time, psychological and emotional trauma and it is usual for the higher court to uphold the decision of the lower court since it is to the Court's image and benefit to appear to the Public that it is unified, even if it has to be unjust. The judges are all birds of the same feather.

What makes the witness(es)' version of the incident accurate? It is scientifically established that what an individual represents to have seen is just that – her/his version of what she/he **believes** she/he saw and/or heard, not what was objectively observed and accurately reported. An individual who is called to bear witness also has her/his personal prejudices and has the opportunity to present a biased version of the incident, especially when it concerns race, religion, ethnicity and gender. She/he did not set out, at the onset of her/his day, to accurately record the behaviors of all involved in the incident. Her/his becoming a witness is incidental and, thus, cannot be accurate. It is not like a scientist who is objectively observing and recording all the outcomes of an experiment. Other scientists are also required to conduct the exact same experiment under the exact same conditions and objectively and accurately record and report her/his findings before the outcome(s) are accepted as fact(s). Testimonies of incidental and/or circumstantial witness(es) cannot be facts but they are treated as such by the Court, especially when they are Police "witness(es)."

The current system allows the accused to hire the services of a lawyer. And, if she/he cannot afford a lawyer, she/he is entitled to a Court appointed lawyer. Whom does the Court-appointed lawyer represent? What is the legal ability of the lawyer appointed by the Court to represent the legal rights (as per the Bill of Rights) of the accused? What prejudices is the lawyer bringing with her/him to the case? And, with the large number of cases before the Court/Judge, is adequate time being given to the pursuit of justice in each individual case? The answer is "No." For these and other reasons the system of "justice" is a farce.

Defendants who have more financial resources have access to more skillful and knowledgeable lawyers. More skillful and knowledgeable lawyers have a greater capacity to acquire a favorable outcome for her/his client(s). Money can, and does, buy justice. If the accused has limited or no financial resources, she/he can expect limited access to the halls and personalities of justice. It is also the public's perception that judges can be bribed, especially by colleagues with whom they attended school and are friends of.

Justice cannot be served or realized in this currently prevailing system.

If Justice is being served, why is it that the Public appears to have little or no faith in the System, as it is currently being administered and operated?

The Italians, the Russians, among other nationalities in the USA, have created "alternative systems" of justice for themselves precisely because the neo-British system, designed by neo-British minds, has failed to achieve any justice, or semblance of justice, under objective scrutiny, in spite of the fact of the existence of the Bill of Rights in the USA. The Bill of Rights does not ensure or guarantee the Rights of all citizens equally. And, this being the case, a new system of justice is required if we are to arrest the caucus and dominance of crime in Society.

This is why the majority of humankind has invented, throughout history, past and present, a just God to whom they appeal and pray. May God help us all in the pursuit of fair and just societies without which said fairness and justice murders and petty crime cannot stop. And while judges preside over case(s) of murder and petty crime, by far, the greatest criminal and immoral act is the stealing of entire elections and the overthrow of legitimately, democratically, and popularly elected, governments by self-proclaimed "super" powers. And while individuals are chastised for petty crimes, known murders parade as leaders and Hon. Presidents!

It is quite obvious to me that the administration and delivery of Justice in the USA (and elsewhere) is a hoax. The evidence is all in in the USA. More Afro-Americans are incarcerated, or killed by police, than any other racial/ethnic group – more than their percentage in the general population. Caucasians/Whites is the largest racial/ethnic group in the USA but they populate the imprisoned population disproportionately. Females also populate the prison population disproportionately.

There is abundant evidence to conclude that, in spite of the national Bill of Rights, the many states engage in and practice "state sponsored terrorism" against minorities, especially Afro-Americans. Is the Bill of Rights not applicable to all citizens equally, especially Afro-Americans?

Whose responsibility is it to apply the Bill of Rights equally to all citizens, including all minorities, especially Afro-Americans? This must be the responsibility of the State and the federal governments.

Do these two levels of government enforce the Bill of Rights equally to all citizens at all times?

The answer is "No." With all the resources available, both personnel and financial, to both the State and federal governments, the pertinent question is, "why"? Why is it that all governments, supposedly elected by the people, for the people in a self-proclaimed Democracy, like the USA, cannot apply the Bill of Rights equally to all citizens at all times?

The answer? All levels of governments in the USA, designed by Caucasians/Whites for the political and economic benefit of themselves, is, by design and operation, discriminatory against non-white citizens! This has been (and is still) the purpose of governments – to discriminate and oppress!

Discrimination by itself is not the problem per se. Discrimination becomes the problem because of the existence of the Bill of Rights which, when known, informs the citizenry that its members have "rights" and that all citizens are to be treated equally in the administration and operation of the system of Justice. Let's take an example: if my mother gives a candy to my sister and instructs her to give it to me but I am not aware of this, if my sister does not give it to me, I cannot say that I was cheated. When my mother later informs me that she sent a candy with my sister for me and asks whether my sister gave it to me or not, then I would know that I was cheated by my sister. If there weren't a Bill of Rights in which the "rights" of the citizenry is written, then the citizenry, especially minorities, would not have expected to be treated equally by the said levels of governments that established the said Bill of Rights! If the governments tell us that we have "rights" and that these "rights" are in the Bill of Rights and then the said governments deny us these "rights," to whom can we complain?

Perhaps we would have been better off, both psychologically and emotionally, if there weren't a Bill of Rights! Why have "rights" if these "rights" are not enforced by the levels of government that have had these "rights" enacted? Why make rules if you cannot, or refuse to, enforce these rules. Just picture a home without rules or one in which new rules are made almost daily but never enforced!

The mockery and charade that is labeled "justice" is further complicated and confused (in the USA) because, in the federalist system, each state can make its own laws and does not have to adhere to federally-made laws. If a state adopts a federal law (but it does not have to) only then it is legally obligated to enforce and comply with that law.

We have the current situation of "sanctuary cities." How is it that cities like New York and San Francisco can defy federal immigration laws and harbor and protect illegal immigrants? The Trump administration, with executive order, attempted to deny federal funds to "sanctuary cities" but the Supreme Court ruled this executive order to be unconstitutional! Illegal immigrants are welcomed in NYC! NYC refused to obey federal immigration law and the executive order of the President of the USA! What a legal mess and confusion!

Further, in the USA, we have (a) federal laws, (b) state laws, (c) county laws, (d) city laws, (e) coop laws, (f) homeowners' association laws, some of which are contradictory. And, then, we have The Bill of Rights! Which of these laws are applicable? There is also the United Nations Organization declaration of "human rights!" If this is not a mess, what is? And, year in and year out, each of these levels of government is making more and more laws. There are law libraries housing tons of law books. Judges' rulings and decisions become "precedent law." If one has the money and connections, she/he can be easily exonerated of a criminal act. Can there be "Justice?"

As we have seen recently some states in the USA have legalized marijuana. Prior to this legalization, marijuana was illegal. Tens of thousands of the citizenry were incarcerated for having marijuana in their possession or smoking marijuana because it was illegal. So there is reason to say that the behavior becomes a crime because there is a law against it. With the law(s) the crime is created! Was the Bill of Rights of any use to those who were found with marijuana in their possession when there was a law against it?

To further complicate matter some state have legalized marijuana while others have not done so. So the same act is legal in one state but not in another! So it was with alcohol – "probition" as it was called.

Some localities acknowledge and permit "domestic partner" relationship and same-sex marriages. Other states do not. Here again the same behavior is legal in one state while it is illegal in another in the same USA!

So, what is the use of The Bill of Rights? Why is there a Bill of Rights? What "rights" do we truly have?

Who has the ability and capacity to enforce and apply these "rights" fairly and justly and equally?

There is also the confusion between Religion and State. This further complicates the fair and equal application of the Bill of Rights. The Constitution of the USA dictates "religious freedom" in one of it Amendments. Those males who profess to be members of the Mormon faith as well as those who profess to be Muslims, invoking their "religious freedom" rights may choose to have four (4) wives. Those males, who claim to be Christians or Hindus, by their religion, can have only one (1) wife. In the instance of the state law prohibiting bigamy how will the Mormons and Muslims be judged? Are they to be allowed by the state and federal governments to have four (4) wives because of their religious rights? Or, are the various levels of governments to adjudicate on the basis of its laws?

Muslims affirm that it is against their religion to "gamble." As such, invoking their "religious freedom" rights they are exempted from the fines imposed by the federal government on those who do not have medical insurance. How can this be reconciled? Which laws are to be enforced – the federal laws, or the state laws, or the dictates of each and every religion? How does this conflicting reality allow for the administration of Justice and Fairness in the doctrine espoused in the Constitution and Bill of Rights of the USA that "all men are created equal?"

THE CONSERSVATION OF MATTER:
(Essay #4)

"The notion is that mass, or matter, can be neither created nor destroyed. According to conservation of mass, reactions and interactions which change the properties of substances leave unchanged their total mass; for instance, when charcoal burns, the mass of all of the products of combustion, such as ashes, soot, and gases, equals the original mass of charcoal and the oxygen with which it reacted."

"The special theory of relativity of Albert Einstein, which has been verified by experiment, has shown, however, that the mass of a body changes as the energy possessed by the body changes. Such changes in mass are too small to be detected except in subatomic phenomena. Furthermore, matter may be created, for instance, by the materialization of a photon (quantum of electromagnetic energy) into an electron-positron pair; or it may be destroyed, by the annihilation of this pair of elementary particles to produce a pair of photons."

Since the "original" mass remains constant and is not destroyed what is the validity of the claim that we are "destroying the environment?" What is the scientific basis of this claim?

The original total environmental mass at creation will remain the same in quantity if the law of conservation of matter holds true. Perhaps the composition of matter will change but the total original mass will not.

Perhaps a more accurate statement is that the composition of the earth's environment is changing while the total mass remains constant.

Another dilemma is generated by the equation $E=MC^2$. Who has more energy, a healthy young male of standard body mass or an obese male of four (400) hundred pounds? The four-hundred-pound male has more mass. According to the formula, energy = mass x a constant (the speed of light)^2. Since the four (400 lbs.) hundred-pound male has more mass, am I to conclude that he has more energy? This is not the functioning or observed reality.

I remember the time when the great minds argued that "slash-and-burn" agriculture was detrimental to the local ecosystem and the environment in general. With further studies, however, this claim has vanished from the debate or discussion. I guess they have more fashionable topics to debate and discuss.

I cannot help but give credence to the claim by developing countries that the whole body literature and general alarm of "climate change" is politically motivated. The developed countries used, and continue to use, fossil fuels carelessly and wastefully. These said developed countries are vociferous in their arguments and plentiful in their meetings and rallies against the use of fossil fuels in developing countries. The argument? The developing countries will cause a destruction of the environment. Can the environment be truly destroyed since matter is neither created nor destroyed?

I guess that the developed countries are asking that the developing countries not opt on a path to development. Development calls for a lot of energy. And, energy sources include fossil fuels. Developing countries must, by necessity and need, use fossil fuel to fuel their infrastructural development and transportation need.

What is also ironical is that the developed countries own the technology to mine for and process fossil fuels. So why is it that they do not want to make these energy sources available and accessible to the developing countries? The developing countries are available markets for energy and energy mining machinery. The exaggerated emphasis on climate change as a direct result of the use of fossil fuels is clearly politically motivated. There is probably conclusive scientific information about the overuse of fossil fuel, but this overuse is not attributable to developing countries. They can't afford to waste fuel. The exaggeration is also politically motivated.

The developed countries own and operate a media that is highly developed, sophisticated, subtle, and pervasive and is applied for the profit motive and the propagandization of a western, youthful culture. With this media infrastructure and mature fossil fuel technology the developed countries are utilizing scientific data to confuse the true cause and nature of environmental changes brought about on planet earth by them. Because of their insufficient knowledge and reckless consumption of energy and their abuse of the resources of the planet, the planet is undergoing some environmental changes. They are then saying that "we" are destroying the environment. Who is the "we?" And, can the environment be truly destroyed?

IS THE NEW GOD – "DEMOCRACY?"
Essay #5

We can start with the God-kings who were bullies, really! Up until Henry VIII of England "religion" was the "God." The God-kings

had to get permission from the God of religion, Roman Catholic religion, "His Holiness The Pope," to do what they wanted to do, even to get married or to get a divorce. Henry VIII broke away from Catholicism, the controlling dogma of the Pope's power, so as not to have to get a divorce to allow him to marry Catherine of Argon. If the Pope had granted him the divorce he wanted, he would not have had to send his then wife to the gallows. It was the Pope who caused the death of Anne Boleyn, *(left. Photo: Wikipedia.org)* Henry VIII fifth wife. (Symbol of the "God-kings" – monarchs (crown above) Source: google.com)

Henry VIII then created a new God-religion, the Church of England, and named himself as the head of this new church. He made himself the new God. As the head of the Church of England he consolidated his divine right to rule. He no longer had to get the Pope's permission or consent to do whatever pleased him or whatever he desired. He could have extended his bullying wherever and whenever he so pleased! He was truly the God-king.

The Pope was the representative of God on earth; essentially The Pope was the earthly God. It was the Pope who divided up the western hemisphere, the "new" world, among the vying God-kings reigning at that time. Religion was God! And in the name of this God, the Crusade dominated life and war in Europe, which led to the slaughtering of millions in the then world known by Europeans.

Or, we can go further back to be reminded of the time when folks had Gods of War. God was war and wars were fought for War Gods! Folks prayed to and worshiped their War Gods. War was worshiped as a God!

Today Muslims all over the world, like the Christian Crusaders then, are at war all over the world in the name of and for their God-religion.

The Pilgrims fled from England because of persecution. The God-Religion and the reigning God-king of that time did not tolerate any other type of God-religion. Any other God-religion was a direct threat to his kingdom and his god-like stature. "Some 100 people, many of them seeking religious freedom in the New World, set sail from England on the Mayflower in September 1620. That November, the ship landed on the shores of Cape Cod, in present-day Massachusetts." (www.history.com)

Going forward a new "God" had come into being. That new "God" was capitalism. Capitalist countries, in the name of this new "God," waged war incessantly to impose their colonial dominance one against the other. The capitalist countries waged war on fascist countries. The capitalist "God" was victorious and Hitler, Mussolini, and Franco lost and have been relegated to permanent historic ignominy. Though a new name was allotted to the new "God" the majority of the populace of the capitalist countries continued to worship their God-religion – Christianity.

Capitalism led to plantation agriculture. Plantation agriculture required labor. The need for labor in the "new world" led to the ignominious institution of slavery. Again, the capitalist countries that engaged in institutionalized slavery were "Christian" nations. Their God-religion allowed them to enslave other men and women, to ill treat them beyond what is humanly possible, so that they can make more and more money.

Money was the next "God" that came into being. We have to make a lot of money by any means possible. Though slavery was "abolished" freed laborers were paid the barest minimum and were worked for long hours in deplorable work conditions to make money. Wars are created and engaged in to make money. With impunity and absolute power Money, the new "God" reigned/reigns supreme. We worship money, the new "God." (Symbol of Money, above): Source: google.com. Below: Symbol of "Democracy" Source: google.com

Now the new "God" is "Democracy." The idea of "democracy" came out of the Renaissance. This was the gift of the French to the new and old world. The God-kings had to be overthrown. They were bullying too much and too many.

They were bullying the populace for more and more money and for more and more self-indulging power.

The very few owned all the land and all the money. In the name of the new "God", democracy, wars were/are fabricated.

The very few decide that all countries must have "democracy" whether they are ready for "democracy" or not.

Korea must have "democracy". Vietnam must have "democracy". China must have "democracy". Cuba must have "democracy". They are to be bombed into acceptance of "democracy". Guyana must have "democracy". If democracy is not the "God" in a country that country is declared to be an enemy of the "God-democracy" countries. Democracy must be the sole "worshipable" "God." Everyone must eat, sleep and breathe democracy. Even if a country has a good relationship with another country that is not a "democratic" country, that country, by association, is declared an enemy.

The new casualties of "democracy" are Egypt, Syria, Iraq, Iran, and Libya – the Middle Eastern Islamic countries. Also, if the government of a country or the population of that country is labeled "communist," that government/country must be destroyed. The dogs of war must be unleashed and there will be no prisoners. "Communism" must not be allowed to spread; it must be contained with the might of the military industrial complex of the capitalist countries.

If one does not worship the majority God-religion, one is an enemy and is to be killed. Christians classify non-Christians pagans and non-believers. Non-Christians are to be killed. Muslims brand non-Muslims infidels and kaffirs. Infidels are to be killed. Countries that are labeled undemocratic or that have a communist friend are to be indiscrimately bombed. The new "God" is democracy and this new "God" is good enough reason to go to war again and again even though the wars are not won! In the name of "Democracy" millions must be murdered just as why millions were/are murdered in the name of "Religion" and in the name and for Money. But we must protect sharks, alligators, bears and other predators while we kill and murder women and children in the name of and for the "God" democracy.

WARS: Why we have them? <u>Essay #6</u>

"Of the past 3,400 years, humans have been entirely at peace for 268 of them, or just **8** percent of recorded history. At least **108 million** people were killed in wars in the twentieth century. Estimates for the total number killed in wars throughout all of human history range from 150 million to 1 billion." <u>www.nytimes.com</u> in an article titled *"What you need to know about wars."*

"At the beginning of 2003 there were 30 wars going on around the world. These included conflicts in Afghanistan, Algeria, Burundi, China, Colombia, the Congo, India, Indonesia, Israel, Iraq, Liberia, Nigeria, Pakistan, Peru, the Philippines, Russia, Somalia, Sudan, and Uganda." <u>www.nytimes.com</u> *"What you need to know about wars."*

"Ongoing conflicts around the world: Major wars, 10,000+ deaths in current or past calendar year. Wars, 1,000-9,999 deaths in current or past calendar year. Minor conflicts, 100-999 deaths in current or past calendar year. Skirmishes and clashes, fewer than 100 deaths in current or past calendar year. Only the locations where the conflicts are taking place, not the warring parties, are coloured. For example, for the war in Afghanistan only Afghanistan itself is

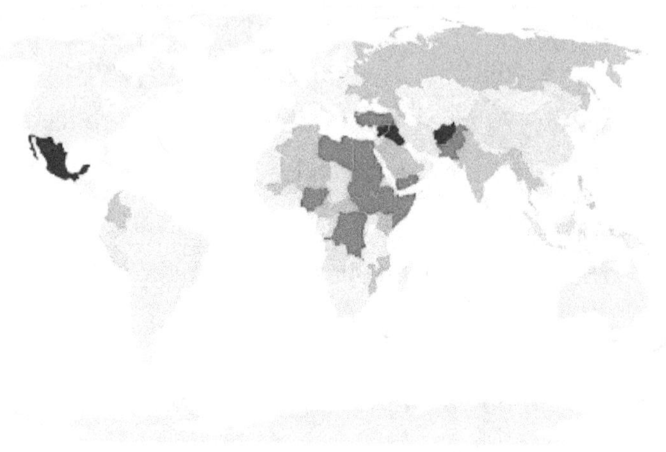

More wars/battles are in the continent of Africa. Africa is the poorest continent of all the continents and more Blacks/Negroes live in Africa than in any other continent. Is this a mere coincidence? Or is this by design? Why are there more wars/battles in the continent of Africa?

Is poverty a result of wars/battles? Or, war/battles is the result of poverty? Does race play a causative role in wars/battles? More Africans are of the Negroid race than any other race. So, there is racial homogeneity in parts of Africa. Comparatively, more Chinese are of the Mongoloid race than any other race. More Indians are of the Caucasian-Aryan sub-racial group than any other racial group. More Europeans are of Caucasian stock than any other racial stock. So there appears to be racial homogeneity in these three continents, generally speaking. Also, more North Americans are of Caucasian stock than of any other stock. In South America there appears to be no easily identifiable single majority racial stock as in China, India, and Africa. So there is global evidence to conclude that wars/battles appears not to have race as a basis for its cause. Where there is racial homogeneity, as in Africa, there are many wars. And where there is racial homogeneity, in China and North America, there are no wars/battles currently being fought.

North America, China and Europe are not labeled "poor" continents or countries. Many South American and African countries are labeled "poor" countries. More wars/battles are fought in Africa and South America. So it appears that, from a global perspective, there are more wars/battles where there is poverty. It appears, on the surface, that people in poor countries engage in wars/battles because they are competing among themselves and their neighbors for "scarce" resources. Why are there currently more wars/battles where there is poverty?

There are 54 countries in Africa today, according to the

United Nations. "Africa is the second-largest and second most populous continent on earth with an estimated population in 2016 of 1.2 billion people. Africa is home to 54 recognized sovereign states and countries, 9 territories and 2 de facto independent states with very little recognition. The UN Population Fund stated in 2009 that the population of Africa had hit the one billion mark and had therefore doubled in size over the course of 27 years." *(Source: www.worldpopulationreview.com)* Is population density a factor in the cause of poverty and, thus, wars/battles?

Continent Populations 2017

Name	2017 Pop.	Growth Rate In %	Pop. Density Per Sq. Km.
World	7,515,284,153	1.0838	57,768
Africa	1,246,504,865	2.4399	42,043
C. America	177,249,493	1.2447	72,208
N. America	363,224,006	0.7389	19,474
Oceania	40,467,040	1.3759	4,768
Europe	739,207,742	0.0389	33,396
S. America	426,548,297	0.9188	24,428
Asia	4,478,315,164	0.9144	144,308

Data Source: www.worldpopulationreview.com

There are 44 countries in Europe today, according to the United Nations. "The overall area that makes up the continent of Europe remains mostly unchanged for thousands of years. What changes most frequently are the dividing lines of the countries that make up the continent. Over time new countries will form and others will split or fade away." Source: www.whatarethe7continents.com. So it is for Africa also.

There are only two (2) countries in North America, the United States of America (USA) and Canada and twelve (12) countries in South America.

We notice immediately that the continents with the larger number of countries have more wars/battles. Or, more wars/battles can be found in the two continents with the larger number of countries – Europe with 44 countries and Africa with 54 countries have more wars/battles than the other continents individually and collectively. This simple fact points to the current reality that politics, the creation of new political boundaries – creation of new countries – is the principal cause of wars/battles.

Population density does not seem to have a strong correlation with wars/battles. Asia with the highest population density in the world (144,308/sq. km.) has the least amount of wars/battles. North America with 19,474/sq. km. has no wars/battles.

As the continents of Europe and Africa are divided up into more and more "independent" countries we can expect more and more wars/battles as new nations are carved out of the older ones. So, this is one reason why we have wars/battles in the world. Perhaps it would have been best that these individual "independent" countries be isolated in their wars/battles with each other. But this is not the current reality. Each of these small countries in Europe and Africa seeks military and other assistance from the wealthy and military equipped countries of the world. Ukraine seeks help from the USA and Syria seeks help from Russia. North Korea is assisted by China while South Korea is supported by the USA. Israel is an ally of the USA but Palestine has no "friend." Palestine is still waiting to be recognized as a sovereign "state" by the USA and Israel. Would Palestine ever be recognized as a sovereign state by Israel and the USA?

"For the past 50 years, Israel has tried to have it both ways: taking the land by planting Jewish settlements on it; and keeping the Palestinians unenfranchised under military occupation, denied either their own state or political equality within Israel (see our/react-text special

report react-text: 1120 in this issue)": Israel's "temporary" occupation has endured for half a century. The peace process that created "interim" Palestinian autonomy, due to last just five years before a final deal, has dragged on for more than 20. A Palestinian state is long overdue. Rather than resist it, Israel should be the foremost champion of the future Palestine that will be its neighbour. This is not because the intractable conflict is the worst in the Middle East or, as many once thought, the central cause of regional instability: the carnage of the civil wars in Syria, Iraq and elsewhere disproves such notions. The reason Israel must let the Palestinian people go is to preserve its own democracy."   Source: The Economist (Magazine) May 20, 2017.

The above paragraph is the most pertinent example that accurately illustrates the issue I am identifying – wars/battles are caused by contemporary world politics which has expressed itself in the creation of two new states, (in this case) Israel and Palestine, endorsed by the UN after WWII. Israel is recognized as a sovereign state but Palestine is not. Because of this political unfairness the war between Israel and Palestine escalates and subsides, like a wave, without an end in sight. The problem was created politically and, thus, the solution is a political solution. There are those who espouse a "two state" solution. This is most ironical for the two states (one recognized as such and the other is not) did not create this political problem which, according to the Economist, is "as many once thought, the central cause of regional instability" – the many wars/battles in the Middle East, Africa.

South Sudan was recently carved out of Sudan as an "independent" nation. There is currently war and famine in South Sudan, a country in Africa. West Sahara, a newly created "independent" country, is claimed by Morocco. West Africa, another newly created "independent" country, was an integral part of the state of South Africa. We can expect war/battles to break out soon – more war/battles in Africa! These are more recent examples of new political boundaries being readied for war/battles.

When a poor country is divided into two new poor countries, each claiming to be "independent," what hope or possibility can there be for economic development? When political action results in division (Israel and Palestine; North and South Korea; North and South Vietnam; Iraq and Kuwait; India and Pakistan) the stage is being prepared for war/battles. "Independent" small countries cannot defend themselves and do not have the intellectual and/or financial capital for development. "Independence" is a choice for war/battles, devastation and exploitation by the wealthy/rich larger nation states.

But wars may have a more useful function. As is quoted from the New York Times above an estimated 150 million to 1 billion people have been killed in wars over a period of 3,400 years of human history. Would the planet Earth have been able to support this estimated 1 billion more had they lived and procreate? It is natural for the Environment to establish equilibrium by any means. Environmental equilibrium does not have to concern itself with morality. When there are too many or too much, some must be removed! Going to war is one way to remove excesses, for "there is a time for peace and a time for war." Plagues, famines and pestilences are occurrences of the contemporary past, keeping population in check.

Now we are having more weather-related "natural" disasters, keeping population in check.

With advances in modern medicine more people are living longer, especially in the developed/rich countries. Apparently, since they have the financial resources and the social support system, they may survive and live a "full" and longer life while those who were born (and more they want and need to live a "full" life remain) in the poor, small and warring countries die earlier. What is the point of living when one does not have the financial resources or the social support system to live, much less to live a "full" life? Death for some ends their need for sustenance, shelter, medicine, procreation, etc. while releasing more resources to those who can afford to purchase what

Nature always seeks equilibrium. The heat from the tropical region is distributed all over the earth. The cold of the North and South Poles mixes with the warmth of the tropics to achieve temperature equilibrium. A cup of hot coffee soon cools when left open. The heat from the coffee dissipates into the cooler atmosphere to achieve temperature equilibrium at the micro level. As surface land sinks to the substratum levels through the process of "subduction" new land is made from materials brought to the surface by volcanic eruptions. This is equilibrium at a macro scale. The same is true for population equilibrium.

When the known world was "small," population level was maintained by/with pestilences, plagues, diseases, and natural disasters, and wars. We can group the various causes of population equilibrium into two groups:

"natural causes" and "unnatural causes." Natural causes would include events of Nature, which result in loss of life, in small or large quantities. Unnatural, or "man-made" disasters, such as wars, also cause population levels to decrease so as to achieve population equilibrium globally. So wars, an invention of man, with Natural Disasters, complete the system with which population equilibrium is achieved globally.

What we notice also is that the victorious armies, usually of men, would rape the women of the conquered/defeated countries. (After WWII many German women married many American GIs; they were not raped) When a culture or country restricts and contains its women with social taboos from mating with males of another tribe, culture or country, or another religion, we can expect invasions and wars. Nature wants the gene pool to be continuously mixed. So when this natural order is in check unnaturally, Nature will cause one group (of men) to invade another group with the hope of mating with the women. In the event that they (the men) do not get to mate with the women, they usually rape them.

We have witnessed what is known as "sexual selection." The females decide with whom they will mate.

When females are prevented from exercising this natural right of sexual selection, a natural behavior, they tend to engage in promiscuous sex. The gene pool must be mixed. In the instances of war the social structures and taboos of the culture are in decline and less rigid and, thus, the females become more at liberty to mate with whom they please. They may even engage in "prostitution" to save their families and relatives from torture and exploitation. In this manner and because the natural order was blocked during the time of "peace" wars allow for open market sex and the naturally intended order of the mixing of the genetic pool.

We have wars as a means of achieving global population equilibrium and as an opportunity for the mixing of the human gene pool, which latter is usually controlled by cultural and social taboos during times of peace. With the wars in Africa/Middle-East hundreds of thousands of women and children are involuntarily migrating to Europe. The men are staying in the devastated countries to fight to their deaths. The women, most naturally, will soon mate with the men in Europe. Some of the children, as they grow to sexual maturity, will certainly mate with European sex partners. The gene pool will be mixed. Nature has a way of getting its way in spite of all the mountains of cultural and social taboos, artificial as they are, set up by humans. We notice (from the chart before) that Europe currently (2017) has the lowest population growth rate – 0.0389 % - and is most in need of an inflow of outside genes to maintain a healthier population and population equilibrium. The wars in Africa/Middle-East are enforcing, serendipitously, Natures purposes. North America has the second lowest population growth rate – 0.7389 % - but accepts legal and illegal immigrants in the millions every year. This ensures the mixing of the gene pool with the millions of interethnic and interracial marriages. (There are many births also outside of any marriage) Nature, I note, does not care whether or not the parties are married, for, marriage, a man made institution, is not required for sex and child bearing. There are currently (2017) no wars in North America.

I note, however, that marriage, a political tool, when used on a grand scale and at the international level, can sometimes result in the redrawing of political boundaries. Marriage was also used in Europe to consolidate small city-states. We have the story of Romeo and Juliet, the "star crossed" lovers, as the universal reference of an attempt by Nature, with love, at a micro scale, to bring about a merging of feuding families. Love, desire and sex motivate intended marital unions.

I will refer to the foregoing as "wars naturally explained" from a political perspective. Additionally, we also have wars that can be naturally explained from an economic perspective as well as from a religious perspective.

As is more noticeable now, even though this has been the reality from the beginning of human history, as monetary wealth, by design, moves up the economic ladder and is secured in banks, the majority of humankind becomes poor and impoverished. This disequilibrium in the acquisition and distribution of the financial resources of the country is a major cause of social unrest, the harbinger of war. When the kings and queens of Europe, for example, were very wealthy and the masses were wretched and poor, there were numerous wars. Those wars resulted in some economic and social changes and some, even for a short time, release of financial resources (the costs of the wars themselves) to the lower stratum of society. Wealth was allowed to trickle back down.

The "New World Order" (it's nothing new, really) is the same reality, only on a global scale. The few of the world (the banks, the Bill Gates, the Bronsons and the like) have amassed so much wealth from the destitute, impoverished masses that there is social unrest and impending wars in all continents, including North America. To say the least there is economic inequality in all countries of the world. This economic inequality is the fermenting yeast for social upheavals all over the world. Civil wars have broken out in Africa, Europe and South America. The Venezuelan economy (an oil producing country) is currently (2017) on the brink of collapse and civil war can soon break out. The situation is very similar in Nigeria, another poor oil producing country. The wealth of the country moves upwards to the very few while the majority of the people remain poor and suffering with daily struggles to get basic human needs.

As a result of this imbalance in the distribution of wealth there are, or will be, wars, which wars will result in both a reduction of the population (especially from among the poor) and a redistribution of some of the wealth from the top to the bottom. This is an attempt at economic equilibrium, even if for a short period of time.

It is interesting to note that the wealthy few of Africa, South America and Asia, and Oceania, having exploited the resources and peoples of these parts of the globe soon migrate to the richer continents of North America and Europe where they will be exploited in turn.

In this manner the wealth of the so-called Third World

countries, because of the social unrest created by unequal economic systems resulting in wars, the collective wealth of the poor continents and countries soon make its way to the richer continents and countries of the world.

When the economic wealth of these poor continents (Asia, South America and Africa) and poor regions of Oceania and the Caribbean was exploited by the European colonial powers, many countries from these parts of the world fought for their "independence" from the colonial powers. These wars for "independence" were attempts to establish economic equilibrium on a global scale. While many countries were able to gain their political "independence" from their colonial masters, they are yet unable to achieve economic independence. In actuality they will continue to be poor because the bulk of their wealth has already been exploited and transported to the European banks. Their achieving political "independence" from their colonial masters is of no economic value to them; their political "independence" translates into allowing their colonial masters to legally neglect them and relieves their masters of any moral obligation to assist them in their incapacity and inabilities to achieve economic independence.

Further, "independence" allows these poor countries to be ravaged further by their own elected citizens who then amass wealth, which wealth they themselves voluntarily transfer, via the banks, to the very same rich colonial continents of North America and Europe. The New Global Order simply creates a new way to perpetuate economic disequilibrium on a global scale. There are more people and more "independent" countries to exploit to make those who were already rich, wealthy and powerful, richer, wealthier and more powerful. The world stage is set for more wars. Perpetual economic inequality and designed disequilibrium are another major cause of wars in our world.

It is further interesting to note that the offspring of the poor is recruited by the rich and wealthy in the many armies of the rich countries of the world to kill, murder, or lay siege upon, their poor parents and "neighbors."

Rich men and women can buy more of everything, including sex. What is the point of having more economic or political power? Men with political and/or economic power soon attract more women or the most sexually desirable women, even if both of them may be married. So, the purpose of acquiring individual economic wealth and/or political power (in the rich or poor countries) is to give the individual more access to more sex. Wealth and/or power may be desirable in and of themselves but, having one or both of them, sure opens up more opportunities for sex and dominance in rich or poor countries. (It is now stated that one in every two hundred males in the world carries the gene of Genghis Khan, the most powerful conqueror/ruler the world has ever seen.) This is the single best example to give creditability to the point I am making.

Complementary political power, and economic means, and religions, are causes of wars. The Moghuls of Mongolia in the north invaded India and imposed Islam upon the Hindus. Some Hindus soon converted to Islam to save themselves from certain persecution or death. During the Crusades (the period of Christian religious wars) Christianity was imposed upon southern Europeans and North Africans. During the colonial period Christianity was imposed upon Muslims and Hindus who were brought from India to work on the sugar plantations. These contracted laborers, even though some of them resisted the onslaught of Christian missionaries, did not engage in any serious military campaign against their Christian "civilizers." Some of them converted to Christianity voluntarily while others were offered employment in exchange for conversion to Christianity.

Today (the 21st Century) the four major religions, Christianity, Islam, Judaism and Hinduism are on a collision course. The Muslim Africa/Middle-East, in particular, is colliding violently with Christian Europe and North America. Muslim Pakistan is poised for full-scale war with Hindu India. Judean Israel is engaged in war with Muslim Palestine. Religions have become a powerful basis for war. Some Muslims in Nigeria are militarily challenging the Christians in authority.

This reality is quite ironical since all the religious preachers preach that there is one God. Yet many of their followers cannot live peacefully with neighbors who do not pray to the same God, by name, as they! They each claim that the other is praying to a different God, and, as such, is their enemy! They go to war to enforce their manner of praying (except Hindus).

Some Muslims of Africa/Middle-East, in particular, are willing to engage others, including other Muslims, as well as non-Muslims, in gruesome wars as a result of their religious beliefs. According to some Muslims, if they sacrifice themselves in the holy war or Jihad, they will be rewarded in haven with seventy-two virgin women with whom they may have sex forever. Comparing this incentive with Christian or Judean or Hindu soldiers who fight for personal monetary compensation, it is not too difficult to understand the relentlessness of the Muslim Jihadists and the willingness of new recruits to become Jihadists. The motivating force is sex, if not in this life, in the after-life.

In any event, political power and/or economic wealth is used, worldwide, to gain access to more sex. Religious figures and religious doctrine may also, even if by promise, provide access to more sex. WARS: why do we have them?

WHO SPEAKS FOR AMERICANS? WHO SECURES THE FINANCIAL INTEREST OF AMERICANS? *Essay #7*

To even attempt to answer one, or both these questions, I must ask a simpler question: "Who is an American?" A simplistic answer is "an individual who was/is born in the USA. " (We must bear in mind that the word "American" refers to those who were/are born in the Americas – North America, South America, and Central America. On the continent of North America, there is the USA and Canada.) The word "Americans" herein used is used incorrectly to refer to folks who were/are born in the USA. Are only those who were/are born in the USA Americans? No. There are those who are naturalized citizens and those who are legal residents (green card holders). Another way to answer the question: "who is an American?" is to say that all those who live in the USA and are legally qualified to vote in state and national elections are Americans. Both US citizens by birth and by naturalization qualify to vote in national and state elections. (Are those who are naturally born citizens and those who are naturalized citizens as well as those who can legally live and work in the USA, all of who pay taxes, Americans? Is a person who is a legal resident, who works and pays taxes and makes social security and Medicare payments not an American?)

Americans pay taxes, make contributions to Social Security and Medicare. Social Security contributions and payments to Medicare are NOT, legally, taxes. The former is for retirement and the latter is for healthcare because of disability and/or living until retirement age and living after retirement age. For those who were born up to 1964 (the "baby boomers") the retirement age was 65. When I started making my contributions to Social Security, the stated retirement age was 65. The government informed me at that time that at age 65 I am entitled to receive my stated Social Security benefits. I am entitled to it and so are all the others who are yet alive – all those who are yet alive in the same cohort. In fact spouses of those who made their 40 or more contributions are also entitled to about half the amount the contributor receives or is to receive even if the two parties have divorced.

The Bush and Cheney gang, speaking for Americans and America's security, they said, raked up a war debt of over 1 trillion US dollars, according to estimates. (No one in the current or past administration has been forthcoming with an "accurate" figure.)

At this time the Obama administration has not yet released the amount of the war debt incurred during his administration. What is aired on public television is that Israel receives (not Americans) three (3) billion US dollars each year in military aid. Egypt receives US$500,000,000. Pakistan received US$500,000,000. These are only three (3) of the countries that are receiving US tax payers dollars in the billions while:

(a) President Obama signed into law a one-year increase in the retirement age from 65 to 66 for my cohort to receive their entitlement of Social Security income. This is a one-year denial of SSI entitlements to millions of Americans who made their individual Social Security contributions. The government of America, the legislative and executive branches, has defrauded the senior citizen of America their only source of income on which they depend for daily existence!

(b) The recipients of Social Security disability income had to wait one and a half year more before they may be eligible for Medicare! Totally disabled Americans, who cannot work, must go another year and a half without access to Medicare.

(c) While Americans are defrauded by the government of America, the said government of America is lavishing billions of dollars of American tax dollars on Jews in Israel, Muslims in Egypt, and Muslims in Pakistan, just to mention a few.

(d) In addition let's not forget that Social Security payments, both SSI and SSD, are taxable!

(e) Further, American children are sitting on the floor in makeshift trailers to attend school.

(f) The Congress refuses to appropriate funds to repair the infrastructure in America.

(g) The Congress of America shuts down the American government and threatens to do so again and again.

Who speaks for America? Who protects American tax-paying workers, American seniors, American children? What is the point of "green-card" holders becoming Naturalized American citizens?

At the same time illegal immigrants can get free medical help while they do not pay any income tax and while they get access to the legal system against American citizens.

Clearly the American government does not speak for or secure the interests of American citizens and American taxpayers.

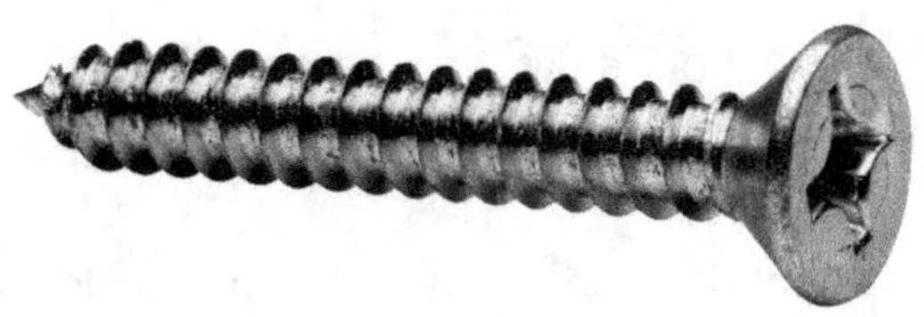

PEACE and CONFLICT: Essay #8

Why this constant looking-back overt time and space by scholars? "To learn from history" is the simple answer. Why the need to learn from history, I ask. So that we do not make the same mistakes again is the usual response! How true are these assertions?

We have engaged ourselves in World War I. And, historians and others have taken several scholarly "look-backs" at WWI with 20th Century tools and "open mindedness." What have we learned? And, if we learned anything, do we apply this new knowledge for a better world? If this new knowledge is applied, who benefits from it? If we learned anything, why then we engaged in WWII soon afterwards?

The major issue for the start of WWI was the "Jewish Problem." The major issue for the start of WWII was the "Jewish Problem." The major issue for the current state of conflicts/wars in the world is still the "Jewish Problem." Why hasn't the so-called "Jewish Problem" not been solved over a period of several decades? Why is there a so-called "Jewish Problem?" Why were the Jews the "problem" for Nazi Germany anyway?

Why were the Iraqis a "problem" for the USA? On the pretext that Iraq possessed weapons of mass destruction (an outright fabrication; a hoax that was perpetrated upon the UN at the UN and the "international" community) President George W. Bush of the USA invaded Iraq. The USA lost the war in Iraq as it has lost the wars in Korea and Vietnam. Why were North Korea and North Vietnam "problems" for the USA? Having spent so much time and money "looking back" at WWI and WWII "to learn" from history, what was learned, and, if anything was learned, why was it not applied to the Afghan war, the Iraq war, the Korean war, or the Vietnam war? Ah, the price others have to pay so that a few may "learn," as they claim!

Why wasn't the Khmer Rouge regime in Cambodia not a "problem" for the USA and/or the "international" community when Pol Pot and his comrades murdered millions of their own citizens? Hitler and his comrades murdered millions of Jews. Were the murdered Jews German citizens? And, even if they were not, what gave Hitler and his comrades the right and authority to attempt to annihilate them in the killing fields and gas chambers?

The USA entered WWI and WWII because of the atrocities meted out to the Jews by the Nazi, among other reasons. But the USA did not intervene in Cambodia in spite of the atrocities meted out to millions of Cambodians by Pol Pot et al. What was learned from WWI and WWII and why was it not applied to Cambodia?

As we continue to look again and again at the holocaust on public television, I wonder as to the need for and purpose of this constant review of this horrific period of human history. Is there a suggestion that, if we air it and view it again and again, we will prevent mass murders by individuals and governments from recurring? Clearly, and factually, this is not the case. We have since had the Korean War, the Vietnam War, The Afghan War, and The Iraq War, in which wars millions more have been murdered and buried in mass graves. What makes WWI and WWII "special" and is to be treated in a "special" way? Is there a suggestion that the Jewish people are the only ones who have a legitimate claim to mass murders and attempted annihilation, and, as such, are entitled to universal sympathy? What is the use and value of sympathy?

Further, are we to accept that issues that are aired on PBS are what truly constitute human historical record? And, that which is not aired or broadcasted in "main stream" media is not a credible record of human history? What constitutes and accurate account of Human history?

It is established academic knowledge that written history, when written by the "winner," is not an accurate account of what happened, how it happened, or why it happened. In fact, there is scientific evidence to state that written history, as the victors wrote it, is falsified history. Hence the continuous need for new research with innovative technology, methodology, and open-mindedness. We cannot just "look back" and repeat the erroneous beliefs as if they are established and scientific facts. When we do so, looking-back is an exercise in futility and an intentional waste of time, money and effort. (A few do benefit monetarily, I note.)

It is a fact that, a group of folks who refer to themselves by/with their religion (like other groups also) and call themselves Jews was scattered all over the then known world. After WWII the victorious Allies (USA and England, in particular) decided that the state of Israel was to be established and that Jews from the Jewish diaspora will have the right to live in Israel permanently if they choose to do so. Israel was carved out from land that belonged historically to Palestinians. The United

Nations Organization ratified the political boundaries of Israel. The boundaries were accepted by many Arab nations even though the King of Saudi Arabia stated that the Jews should be allowed to settle in the USA.

The world stage was set for the conflicts we are currently engaged in – WWIII. Kuwait was carved out of Iraq; North and South Korea were created; North and South Vietnam were created and many more countries were created in Europe. India was divided into Pakistan (east and west) and India (Hindustan) by the booted British at the time of India's "independence". The Pope used to divide up the world among the colonial European powers. This dividing up ensured the conflicts among the colonial countries of Europe.

England, however, did not accept the dictates of the almighty Pope. While other European nations were actively engaged in finding and establishing a trade route to the Far East, England was building up its navy. England was preparing for naval conflict and naval warfare. To undermine the then established structure and status quo (the Pope was the Lord God of heaven and earth) the British government "licensed" privateers to plunder the wealth of the Spaniards, Portuguese, Dutch and French, who were the beneficiaries of the

Pope's benevolence, in exchange for some of the privateers' loot and booty. The British policy was: if British sea captains steal from and/or destroy the Spanish, the Dutch, the Portuguese, and the French en route to Europe from other parts of the world with their galleons laden with gold and other cargo, the British navy will engage in battle to protect/defend them! Pirating was a British licensed activity.

With its policies and navy the British set the stage and agenda for conflict and war while licensing thieves, murders, and despots. The British, descendants of the marauding Vikings who raided, raped and murdered as their way of life all over coastal western Europe, licenses its select citizens to kill any one anywhere in the world and is prepared to defended and protect this select few with the military and diplomatic might of Britain! (PBS in the USA constantly air "murder/mysteries" drama by British writers – murder she wrote - which is most typical and symptomatic of British culture.)

Now the UN is tasked with this role and function and the state of Israel (among others) was established after WWII. Perhaps the thought was that, if an international organization was established and that, if this international organization agreed to the new political boundaries (the boundaries of Israel and other newly established countries), conflicts and war would not continue to be the order of the day. This expectation is not the current reality. There are conflicts all over the world, especially in Europe and the Middle East – the areas where there have been conflicts and wars for centuries! In addition we now have the Israeli and Palestinian conflict/war, the civil war in Syria, among others, in constant view and review on TV in our living rooms.

The UN has failed to enforce the boundaries it had accepted in the case of Israel and Palestine. Why is the UN unable or unwilling to enforce the political boundaries that were established for Israel and Palestine? Why is it that the rest of the world, the so-called "international community" cannot enforce the boundaries that was agreed upon and established by the UN and the "international community?"

This inability or unwillingness is the cause of the many conflicts all over the world and it also causes serious doubts about the UN and other "international" organizations' ability to prevent conflict(s) as is their stated purposes. International organizations have failed to keep the world safe and conflict free.

In fact, upon deeper analysis, with the evidences of the state of the world's affairs, it is quite clear that the UN and other "international" organizations are the cause of the conflicts and wars now evident in the world, especially citing the conflict/war between Israel and Palestine.

Israel continues to build settlements on land that the UN demarcated as belonging to Palestine. And, upon the Palestinians defending their sovereign rights, which sovereign rights were endorsed by the UN, with what meager means that are available to them, the "international" community brands them "terrorists!" Why aren't Israelis branded "terrorists"?

Now Russia has eyes on land in the Ukraine and China is building up land in the South China Sea! The UN and the "international" community are engaged in a war of words and strategies, diplomacy, as it is called, against Russia and China.

What if, to retaliate, Russia or China decides to support the Palestinians against the Israelis, or, say, India joins in in this incapacity or inability of the UN to develop a peaceful settlement to this cancer of the world? Russia has opted to come to the assistance of Al-Assad of Syria. Would China, or India, be willing to render assistance to the Palestinians since the USA supports Israel in spite of the fact that Israel violates the UN agreed upon Israeli/Palestinian border(s)?

India, of course, will not. Why am I so sure? I am sure because, according to an Indian student in one of my classes, Indians like to take and take and take, and having taken as much as they can possible get, they then look around to see what else there is to be taken and take it. They do not stand up for justice and fairness, especially not for some one else or another country. Perhaps the Indians are wise and have learned from looking back in history. Or, perhaps, Indians are spineless and, like yet another of my non-Indian Caribbean student declared, Indians are like cockroaches: they live in constant fear in cracks and crevices darting out only to feed and then instantly disappear from whence they suddenly appeared.

Or, maybe, India knows its weaknesses and has decided that it is ill prepared because of its meager means, lack of political and moral will, or social psychology. In any event India can be very well afraid, like the lowly small fish in the drying pond upon which the soaring eagle preys. The natural order is predation and the eternal struggle is between predator and prey.

Life is predatory. Maybe India refuses to make a prey of itself voluntarily. Or, maybe India does not see itself as a "world" power and, as such, does not wish to participate in the dance of death on the world's stage. India has been for thousands of years (except for periods of British and Moghul domination.)

The fact remains, however: no country or "coalition" of countries has evidently decided to offer support or come to the assistance of besieged Palestine – even the devil is said to have friends but, Palestine, apparently, has none. Why is this so?

This unfairness in words and deed by the UN and the "international" community further exacerbates the tensions created by them. It makes clear that: even though the stated purpose of the UN and the "international" community is world peace, their practices of unfairness, when dealing with all countries, result in perpetual conflicts and wars all over the world.

The purpose of the UN and the "international" community is to ferment conflicts and wars, especially among the poor and developing countries of the world. This is the surest way to keep the poor and developing countries poor and to reduce any explosive population growth in these countries so that they can never become a threat to the "world powers" that be.

I am sure that India and China will be the next targets since these are the two most populous countries in the world. Conflict with China is being brewed right now. If China is to engage in a military battle, most of its recently acquired wealth will be devastated and millions of its soldiers and civilians will die. China will return to the state and status of a "developing" nation with a depleted military and an economy in disarray. The irony is that China is a member of the UN and the so-called "international" community! On whose side will the UN and the "international" community intervene? Would Russia, the USA, England and India form a military "coalition" against China?

After China is devastated, even if India joins the "coalition," Indian will be the next target for political rhetoric, rebuke and destruction. Pakistan is armed with nuclear weapons from the USA and the tension between Pakistan (a piece of India that was separated from India at the time of India gaining its "independence" from Britain) and the-now India is hot and palpable. A military conflict was set in place at the time of the dividing of India into Pakistan and India.

Now Pakistan, which called itself east and west Pakistan, is divided into Pakistan and Bangladesh. So, India has enemies in the east in China and in Bangladesh and in the west and north in Pakistan. The "international" community can easily target India's gains after its "independence" for destruction and devastation. India is a member of the UN but not the UN Security Council; China is. India has not annexed any land or territory of another country, like Israel. Israel remains the closest ally of the USA while it is in clear violation of the UN established boundaries with Palestine.

If India were to invade Pakistan and/or Bangladesh to acquire land that rightfully belongs to India, on whose side will the USA and the "international" community be? Would the USA support India's right to its land, since India will be seeking possession of its own land, which land was divided by Britain? The USA supports Israel even though Israel continues to build new settlements on land that belongs to the Palestinians. Would the USA and the "international" community remain neutral if India attempts to take possession of its land now in the control of and known as Pakistan or Bangladesh? The British left a cocked gun. Who will pull the trigger?

Can China or India impose sanctions against a sovereign nation as the USA has done against Cuba and Iran, to name a few? Each nation is, according to the UN charter, entitled to "self-determination." Why must the USA, Russia, China, Israel, India, Pakistan, and North Korea have nuclear weapons but not Iran, or Cuba? When Cuba chose to be "friendly" with the then USSR, the USA placed an embargo, another word for siege, on Cuba, which it has kept in place for over fifty years. How were the Cuban people to live? Why hasn't the USA placed an embargo on China, which is labeled a communist country with a one-party system of government, just like Cuba? To the contrary, China enjoys "preferred" trading partner status with the USA! Apparently, only China may enjoy the right to self-determination without retaliation from the "international" community.

Europe is now faced with the refugee crisis. Hundreds of thousands of refugees pour into European countries from Syria, Pakistan, Afghanistan, Bangladesh, and African countries. They are being forced to leave their families, friends and familiar surroundings for the great unknown without visas or permits. They are willfully and knowingly violating the political boundaries of many European countries. Why are they all taking this calculated risk? Why aren't the UN and the "international" community able to address the causes that force these hapless individuals from their homelands? Why can't the UN and the "international" community broker "peace" in, say, Syria, for example?

In the conflict/civil war in Syria the "rebels" or "freedom-fighters" are supported by the USA while the President, Al-Assad and his government, are propagated by Russia. This civil war is a war for Democracy – a desire by the "rebels"/"freedom-fighters" to overthrow the traditional ruler, Al-Assad. In addition to the hundreds of thousands who have fled to Europe, unknown hundreds of thousands have been killed, murdered, or gassed to death - all for Democracy, a western concept of government. Is Democracy the answer to the conflicts/wars in the world or is it the true cause? Is Democracy the only form of government?

As we look at the current conflicts/wars in the world we notice a salient fact: the USA and Russia are involved in them, in one way or another.

Why is it that the USA and Russia are involved in perpetuating the conflicts/wars and why is it that the UN is not having any noticeable and useful effect? The obvious answer is that the USA and Russia are military powers with insatiable capacity to wage wars on the world's stage. The UN, on the other hand, does not have its own military, which it may use to enforce agreements among nations.

The USA and Russia, and now China, have usurped the function and purpose of the UN; they have rendered the UN useless or wish to control it as a master owns and controls her/his poodle. There is conflict at the UN.

Why then do the hundreds of small nations attend and participate in the United Nations Organization? Why do they not separate themselves from this powerless man-made entity? Membership is voluntary. Why stay in the UN only to perpetuate its ineffectiveness? Why not leave it?

In addition to the UN there is the British Commonwealth, another useless and powerless entity. Countries that gained their "independence" from Britain had to become members of the British Commonwealth. Ok, they had to become members at the time of gaining independence. Why do they elect to remain members of this entity, which does not have any publicly noticeable use or positive impact on the lives of the peoples of these "independent" countries? According to the UN charter each country has a right to self-determination.

So, since "independent" countries, on the surface, appear to choose to belong to the UN and some to the British Commonwealth, it is fair for me to say that, countries, like individuals, wish to "belong" to something bigger than themselves, just to say that they are members. Even if the organization to which they belong is unproductive or is unable to fulfill its charter, purpose and/or stated mission, they still want to "belong" because the organization's uselessness is of no concern to them.

Every time there is a UN meeting in New York representatives of small/poor and large/rich nations must find the means to be present to "represent" their countries at this entity that is nothing but the battle ground for the so-called "super" powers. They attend to be dominated and or to be bullied by the rich and powerful. The poor citizens of these small/poor countries have to foot the bill for their "representatives" to attend the party, year in and year out. What benefits accrue to the poor of the world after their representatives attend meetings here, then meetings there, meetings at home, and meetings God knows where? At least the elected few, hopefully, do get to indulge themselves at the expense of the poor and the destitute while the rich and powerful acquire and vie for more influence over the said poor and war-torn wretched masses of the world.

As if the UN and the British Commonwealth are not enough toothless poodles, there is NATO, the G-20 and the G-7. Was NATO of any use to the problem in Ukraine? Was NATO of any use in the many wars in the small European countries? With NATO, the G-20, and the G-7 why isn't there peace in Europe, a "mature" continent. People have lived in Europe for quite some time, and, as such, it is fair to say, and expect, that these "civilized" peoples have had some time to iron out their real and perceived differences. This is not the reality, however. Europe is now divided into numerous fiefdoms, not unlike the warring city-states of the Middle Ages. These fiefdoms do relish their right to engage constantly in wars and to drag the rest of the world (WWI, WWII, and now WWIII) into their beastly brutalities while yet claiming to be the most "civilized." Perhaps, "civilized" means engaging in constant murder and mayhem!

Since there is the UN, why the need for NATO or the G-20 or the G-7, especially so since countries that are members of NATO, and the G-20, and the G-7, are also members of the UN? One cannot but impute surreptitious intentions and motives by these organizations. Is it their purpose to undermine the proper functioning of the UN so that they can wield power, influence and control?

Well, they have armies ready to be deployed on labeled "wrong-doers", labeled "wrong-doer" for the same or similar act of the "powerful" countries. Many a times the labeled "wrong-doers," the bad guys, did nothing against any country; they are just defending their right to their land and their right to "self-determination" as is guaranteed by the UN charter. Is it really guaranteed? Who can, or will, enforce this expressed "guarantee?"

In addition to these well-known organizations of the world there are numerous small and un-influential regional organizations, which also schedule meetings, which "elected" officials must constantly attend at the expense of the poor.

Would the answer be to create a new "international" organization, one in which the criteria of power, authority, and influence would rather be high moral and ethical standards of statesmanship and not money and bullying? Would a new organization be able to achieve its stated purpose and mission? Or its mission and purpose would be undermined by the rich and powerful as is the current reality? Would a new international organization be willing and able to treat all its members with the same and uniform policies and practices? Or would it allow some to literally get away with murder?

What tools and mechanisms can it equip itself with to fairly and justly enforce its universal agreements? Who may become members of a new "international" organization? What will be the criteria of membership? Who will set the criteria of membership?

Looking back at the time of India being "granted" its "independence" by the British when "Lord" Mountbatten asked Gandhi that they, the British, be allowed to leave "in dignity" and Gandhi agreed, and at the time when South Africa was "granted" its "independence" under the leadership of Mandela, I notice one major difference: Gandhi did not see it fit to be either the President or Prime Minister of India; Mandela agreed to be the President of "independent" South Africa. This is how and when Gandhi/India won and lost at the same time with the same event.

Gandhi, a British trained lawyer, first went to South Africa. While there, he challenged British authority. In India, however, he made a false and deadly move in the chess game of booting out the oppressive British when he agreed to Mountbatten's request to allow them, the British, to leave "in dignity" and by not being "independent" India's first President. Gandhi, seeming to have acquired the right to make his last move as the opposing, but British trained chess master, against the British, gave the last game away to the British. Had Gandhi forced the British out of India with ignominy, even as they treated many millions of people all over the world, they would not have left with face to face the world again. But "no": Gandhi wanted to show that he was a "gentleman" and a "statesman" of "higher" and "better" moral standing and character; he did not want to kick the enemy when the enemy was "down."

If Gandhi were to have been the President of "independent" India, the British would not have had the opening to divide India and create a wound that has festered and widened like the Grand Canyon and become a constant threat of war between the-now India and Pakistan. Mandela, as President of "independent" South Africa, did not provide such an opening to the departing British. The British saw a clear opportunity to "loose" and to "win" with the same chess move and, rightfully so, they took it. The "Muslim" problem was created and used to divide India and the stage was set for conflict/war yet again by the British who were allowed to leave India "in dignity" by Gandhi! What dignity can there be in conflict and war that is created by those who claim to have and want "dignity?" Now we have both a

"Jewish" and "Muslim" problem in the world. Is religion the true and real problem of/in the world?

What can be learned here? I may say that one can "win" and "loose" with the same stroke, with the same move; loosing and winning is the outcome of the stroke or move not the stroke or move itself. The move can be a false move, the outcome of which can be detrimental to the mover, because the game goes on and does not end with this last and "final" move: the opponent has not given up even though she/he has lost her/his "king"; the opponent keeps herself/himself engaged even though she/he is not to be seen at the playing table – she/he is developing counter strategies and a stronger arsenal.

Conflicts and wars become self-perpetuating. How about the USA's military engagements in all the wars since it became a free nation, self-perpetuating? How about Russia? If China engages, would China perpetuate wars?

IN THE MINDS OF WOMEN AND MEN THE COURSE IS WRIT

AND THE COURSE IS CONFLICT

FOR CONLICT IS NATURAL AS THE RISING SUN

AND, PERHAPS, THIS IS HOW THE GODS HAVE FUN!

The nature of life is: us against them and they against us. It is NOT about who is right, or wrong: it is about opposing or resisting. For each opposing side naturally believes and feels that it is right, just as in the her/his pointless battles: she believes and feels that she is right and he believes and feels that he is right, even though there is no right or wrong in life but only a judge's **opinion** as to such! Who is the judge? Opposing creates strength and balance and conflicts lead to war and war leads to progress! From death and destruction, new life: from life, death and destruction, and ....so life continues! After the Great Fire of London, London was rebuilt to become a bigger and better city with much better sanitation and hygiene. So too the city of Chicago in the USA! After natural forests fires we witness an explosion of growth of new plants and a regeneration of life!

By and because of its ineffectiveness in that it has failed to accomplish the prescriptions of its own charter the UN is defunct. As is in nature where we find new life growing out of the dead and dying, it is time for a new organization. But before we design a new organization let us see why the UN has failed to achieve world peace and prevent conflict so that we may make structural improvements.

The UN has, as its main body, the general assembly: a scheduled meeting of all its members, each member being usually represented by the member-country's president or prime minister. What happens at the General Assembly? Member countries' representatives sit and listen to each other, each trying to persuade the other that its case or approach or solution is the "right" way to go forward. Looking back, if the ways, approaches, or solutions that were selected because they were the "right" way, why then the UN did not achieve the dictates of its charter?

After time and other resources are wasted in the General Assembly the matter, at least some of them, go to the Security Council. The world's "super" powers sit on the Security Council. Each "super" power has veto rights, which it exercises at its own personal whims. In essence, then, if any member of the Security Council does not agree with what was decided at the General Assembly with respect to international "security," that member can exercise its veto causing the matter to die!

Recently the USA (2016) decided not to use its veto power to kill the General Assembly's resolution that Israel is in violation of the border between Israel and Palestine. The resolution stands. If the USA had exercised its veto power, the resolution would have been dead. The General Assembly's decisions/resolutions are subject to the Security Council's veto power of individual Security Council member(s). Thus, simply, but effectively, the majority decision/resolution is denied by the minority. When individual member(s) of the Security Council does not get its way, that member may withhold its funding to the UN. Without this funding the mission and functions of the UN is contained and controlled by the few, like a dog by its master!

This defect in the design of the UN's organization structure needs to be corrected with a better and nonrestrictive, no-minority-control structure.

A mixture of very small/poor and very large/rich nations is a designed recipe for disaster in any organization. The large/rich countries vie for influence and control of the Organization and the mission/functions of the Organization is lost or forgotten in the to-be-expected self-defeating conflicts for control of the Organization. This needs to be corrected.

The location of the UN headquarters in New York City gives unfair advantages to the large/rich countries because the small/poor countries can ill afford the cost of traveling to and doing business in NYC: the poor must compete against the rich!

Any new organization design must correct the aforementioned deficiencies of the UN. Future organization designs will address and correct any future organizational deficiencies.

Going forward there is a need to abandon the UN. "Independent" countries should band themselves together in the OSS – *The Organization of Sovereign States.* The primary purpose of the OSS is to protect and defend the sovereign integrity of each or any of its members against any country, be it a member country or a non-member country. Independence means, first and foremost, sovereignty and territorial integrity. We must select a "now-time" at which time the borders of all countries will be set, respected, and respected by all. We cannot keep looking back and looking back to settle border disputes. How far back must we go?

If a country keeps looking backwards, it cannot go forward. If we keep looking backwards, we will always find that, at one time or another, the current boundaries were different. We must accept boundaries at an agreed upon time, agree to the boundaries at that agreed-upon time and be prepared to move forward.

The second (2nd) purpose of the OSS is to aid the poorest of its members with development aid. To do this the OSS must establish and organize *The OSS Development Bank.* A three-member Board of Trustees, who will be nominated and appointed at/by the OSS General Assembly to serve for a term period of three (3) years, will recruit and hire a President, a Secretary and a Treasurer to operate the *OSS DEVELOPMENT BANK.* The Board of Trustee will supervise the OSS DEVELOPMENT BANK. The Board of Trustee will be selected and appointed by the General Assembly. There shall be three individuals on the Board of Trustees of the OSS Development Bank. The OSS Development Bank will make 10-year-term loans to member countries, giving priority to poorer (Tier I) member countries. Tier I members shall be charged the lowest interest rate for the first 10-year term. Tier II member countries will have second priority to Development Funds and will be charged a slightly higher interest rate than Tier I member countries. Tier III member countries shall be the principal investors in the OSS Development Bank and shall have third priority to Development Funds. Tier III member countries shall pay open-market competitive interest rate.

Tier I, Tier II, and Tier III member(s) shall NOT be limited to borrowing Development Funds from only the OSS Development Bank – they may borrow from any source and use OSS Development Funds as matching funds to secure additional financial guarantees for development projects. The OSS Development Bank may borrow development funds (not operational funds) from any rich country and/or seek grants from international agencies and foundations, public and private. International money managers may be encouraged to invest capital in the OSS Development Bank. The OSS Development Bank may lend capital to governments of member countries, private banks with their HQ in member countries, which funds must be used to fund development projects (existing & new), and can lend directly to businesses/individuals that have their HQ in member countries or who are bona fide citizens of member countries. It may also lend to NGOs, both for profit and not-for-profit, that is registered in member countries. The OSS Development Bank can have branches in any/all member countries over time. The OSS Development Bank can partner with individuals and/or small business entities in the mortgage banking industry in developed countries. This will bring in substantial revenue to finance development projects in OSS member countries.

The third (3rd) purpose of the OSS is to research and establish an "open market/fair trade" **OSS Community Market** among its member countries based upon geographical regions and an inventory of goods, produce, and services in the to-be established OSS Community Markets.

The OSS will NOT have a "veto -power" organizational structure, like the UN. The OSS will have a single stratum of power – the OSS General Assembly. The General Assembly shall be the sole and only decision-making body and shall meet every consecutive year, not every year. Meeting every year is too burdensome. The OSS Board of Executive Directors and General Manager shall execute the decisions, pertaining to Programs & Projects, of the General Assembly. The OSS Secretariat shall be under the direct supervision of the Secretary General and the Secretariat shall concern itself with member-countries relations and the conduct of the General Assembly Meetings as well as overall administration. The OSS Secretariat shall be managed and operated by the Secretary General of the OSS who shall be appointed by the General Assembly for a period of four (4) years with one (1) renewable term for a consecutive time period of no more than eight (8) years. The salary and other terms of employment shall be set by the General Assembly. An Interim Committee of five (5) consultants shall organize the First General Assembly Meeting. The General Manager will also be appointed by the General Assembly for an initial term of four (4) years and may serve, by repeated appointment, for three (3) consecutive terms for a total of no more than twelve (12) years. The General manager must have at least an MBA or, like the Secretary General, must possess a graduate degree in management and planning or management/planning. No PhDs; these are teachers in academia.

The OSS Board of Executive Directors shall oversee the affairs and functioning of the OSS Operations. The Board of Executive Directors will be elected at the first General Assembly Meeting of the OSS. The Board of Executive Directors will decide upon all staffing patterns and titles and the salary for each title with recommendations from the General Manager. The Board of Executive Directors shall set the salary and other terms of employment of the General Manager. The Board of Executive Directors and the General Manager shall each report to the General Assembly at General

Assembly Meetings. The Board of Executive Directors shall hire, from the private sector, appoint and empower a three-member **OSS Evaluations & Review Committee.** This Evaluations & Review Committee shall conduct evaluations and review the functioning of all OSS operations and projects and report directly to The Secretary General and the Board of Executive Directors once every two-year. The E&R Committee may make succinct recommendation(s) direct to the General Assembly at General Assembly Meetings for approval and implementation.

The Secretariat of the OSS shall be in a country in Africa (the poorest) and the Operations HQ of the OSS shall be in a country in the Caribbean (the poorest) and the HQ of the OSS Development Bank shall be in a country of South America (the poorest). The Board of Executive Directors shall be housed in the Operations HQ in the Caribbean.

ORGANIZATION CHART OF THE ORGANIZATION of SOVEREIGN STATES (OSS)

THE GENERAL ASSEMBLY

THE SUPREME BODY OF THE OSS: MEETES EVERY TWO YEARS

THE SECRETARIAT and THE OFFICE of THE SECRETARY GENERAL

THE OSS DEVELOPMENT BANK BOARD of TRUSTEES

THE BOARD of EXECUTIVE DIRECTORS Housed In

OPERATIONS HQ

THE GENERAL MANAGER and

OSS OPERATIONS **STAFF**

EXTERNAL AUDITORS SHALL REPORT TO THE GENERAL ASSEMBLY BI-ANNUALLY and MEMBER-COUNTRIES ANNUALLY

THE EVALUATIONS & REVIEW COMMITTE

FEATURES of THIS ORGANIZATIONAL STRUCTURE:

- Effective Administration/Efficiency
- Separation of Administration from Operations
- Simplicity
- No Redundancy
- Less Bureaucracy
- Lower Operating Costs
- Separated Evaluations and Review

The Secretary General shall appoint **the external auditor(s)** who will audit the books of the OSS Development Bank, the Secretary General/Secretariat and the Operations HQ. The External Auditor(s) will report to the General Assembly bi-annually and member-countries annually.

The Secretary General shall schedule General Assembly Meetings bi-annually as follows:

(a) in the 1st instance, in a country in Africa which may or may not be the African country where the Secretariat is located;

(b) in the 2nd instance in a country of South America which may or may not be the South American country where the OSS Development Bank is located;

(c) in the 3rd instance, in a country of the Caribbean which may or may not be the Caribbean country where the Operations HQ is located.

This pattern shall be repeated every six (6) years. The country shall be selected by the Secretary General at least six (6) months before the scheduled General Assembly Meeting date and all member-countries and Operations HQ and OSS Development Bank, the E&R Committee, and the External Auditors must be notified at a minimum of six (6) months prior to the date of the scheduled General Assembly Meeting. The General Secretary is specifically responsible for this notification task and shall have proof thereof to present to the scheduled General Assembly Meeting which proof shall be accessible by the public for viewing and copying.

The fourth (4th) function of the OSS is to identify individuals and/or organizations, public or private, and government(s) of member countries that exemplify, to the highest level of achievement(s) possible, the values/mission of the OSS, for recognition and award at the bi-annual General Assembly Meetings. The Secretariat staff, under the direct supervision and agreement of the OSS Secretary General, shall decide upon the specific criteria and categories for the awards.

The OSS Secretariat, under the supervision of the Secretary General, is specifically tasked with this responsibility. There shall be no more that twelve (12) recipients/awardees at each bi-annual General Meeting; there may be less. Each awardee shall receive a substantial plaque, a certificate on durable paper and a durable designed button/broach, which shall identify the recipients as proudly belonging to this exclusive group of OSS awardees. The Secretary General and Secretariat staff, from competitive bids, shall decide upon the actual designs.

The Secretary General shall schedule the **Planning Committee** for Planning Meetings at least once a year. Members of the Planning Committee shall include:

    (a) the Secretary General (1)

    (b) the Executive Board of Directors (5)

    (c) the General Manager (1)

    (d) the Board of Trustees (3)

    (e) the Evaluations & Review Committee (3)

    (f) an invited economist, invited by the Secretary General (1)

    (g) an invited geographer, invited by the Secretary General (1)

    (h) TOTAL: fifteen (15) members.

NOTE: The invited guests may be changed every two-year at the discretion of the Secretary General to give an opportunity for the influx of new ideas and they may be paid a stipend to be set by the Secretary General. They may vote at Planning Meetings sessions only.

The Planning Committee must plan and put in place a coordinated Disaster Response & Relief Agency (DRRA) for each member country under the coordination of the OSS Secretariat. The Secretary General may appoint a planner to assist her/him in the effective and efficient coordination of the OSS DRRA.

The OSS DRRA shall set up, manage and disburse a separate OSS Relief Fund. Each member country shall contribute a separate amount (perhaps 2-3% of GDP annually) to this OSS Relief Fund. The actual formula is to be decided by/at the first General Assembly Meeting. The OSS DRRA may solicit grant funding from international organizations and wealthy private citizens.

TO BELIEVE or TO KNOW? Essay #9

I was at a get-together of friends and associates at a real estate broker's home – in the yard – in the evening in June. He and I were standing and talking when the phone in his kitchen rang. He went to answer the phone. I saw him talking to someone on the phone but I did not hear him. (I later learned that he was talking to my wife. She wanted to know if I was at the "party." He told her that I left two hours with a woman to Atlantic City.)

I had about four (4) bottles of beer. So I thought it best not to leave in that state but to take a nap in my car before I departed. I actually slept off until about 11:00 p.m. After I awoke, I readied myself and left for my home in the Bronx, NY. I had to cross the Whitestone Bridge since I was in Queens, NY at the "party." The bridge was undergoing repairs and there was only one lane open. I arrived home at about 4:00 a.m.! My wife asked me where I was. I told her what I stated above. She said that she did not believe me.

The next morning I went downstairs, as usual, to have breakfast with her. She did not make any breakfast. She was just sitting at the table. I asked her what was the matter. She replied with, "I want a divorce!"

"What?" I exclaimed querulously.

"I want a divorce," she repeated flatly.

"Why?" I asked in disbelief at what she was saying.

"You went to Atlantic City with a woman last night and now you are here like a saint. I want a divorce."

"I told you what happened last night," I replied in disbelief. "What makes you think that I went to Atlantic City with a woman last night?" I wanted to know.

"Your friend where you were supposed to be told me so", was her indignant and affirmative reply.

"And you believe him and not me?" I wondered in more disbelief. "He must have been joking with you. You know how he likes to joke around with you for a laugh."

"No! I believe him," she said with absolute finality. "I want a divorce!"

President George W. Bush of the USA declared to the world that he believed that President Saddam Hussein of Iraq had "weapons of mass destruction." Colin Powell, Secretary of State of the USA, addressed the United Nations to advance this belief showing a black-and-white photograph of a stack of empty pipes as proof. President George W. Bush ordered the invasion of Iraq. The war of the Middle East was set in motion because of the advocated false belief of the George W. Bush and his administration. There still isn't an exact dollar amount of the cost of the War in Iraq. It is estimated and believed to be more than a trillion US dollars. We do know that thousands of US soldiers lost their lives in this war, which was based upon the belief of President George W. Bush of the USA, which was false. The President and others did not know that President Saddam Hussein possessed weapons of mass destruction, (WMDs), they just choose to believe that he had. He didn't have WMD! This is a classic example of the universal conflict between belief and knowing the fact(s)!

My wife wanted a divorce on the basis of her erroneous belief, which belief was based on a story that was fabricated by my associate. President George W. Bush declared war on Iraq on the basis of his belief based on fabrications of members of his administration. These two instances of facts highlight the power of belief at the micro and macro levels. What wanton destructions are caused by and with peoples' beliefs! Those who choose to "believe" are evidently lazy because they refuse to go after "knowing" the fact and thus fail to differentiate what is fact and what is just an individual's belief(s). Most of what we hear on so-called "main-stream" media is just the belief(s) of the editors of the newscast and is not actual news.

Further instances of the destructive power of "believing" as against "knowing" can be found in the Middle Ages. The Great Plague!

"This was the worst outbreak of plague in England since the black death of 1348. London lost roughly 15% of its population. While 68,596 deaths were recorded in the city, the true number was probably over 100,000. Other parts of the country also suffered. The earliest cases of disease occurred in the spring of 1665 in a parish outside the city walls called St Giles-in-the-Fields. The death rate began to rise during the hot summer months and peaked in September when 7,165 Londoners died in one week. Rats carried the fleas that caused the plague. They were attracted by city streets filled with rubbish and waste, especially in the poorest areas." www.nationalarchives.gov.uk

They did not believe in hygienic and sanitary public conveniences. Wastes bred rats and rats were the cause of the spread of the Plague. They blamed the Plague on the rats, not themselves and their unhygienic and insanitary behaviors.

There was the majority who did not believe that the earth

is "round." A few individuals risked their lives to even believe that the earth is round. Because of their belief they refused to even consider the possibility that the earth is round and that, thus, by sailing due west one can arrive in the east. The belief of the majority held back the exploration of the earth and delayed the discovery of the Americas and the Caribbean.

There are those who still do not believe that Mr. Trump won the 2016 presidential election in the USA in spite of the fact that: "Overall, he won 2,622 predominantly small counties while Clinton won 490, most of which were much more populous. (Those figures may shift very slightly since some states take a long time to certify their results.) Still, the shifts were large enough for a number of pickups. At present count, Trump snagged 220 counties that voted for President Obama in 2012, while Clinton poached 17 that went for Mitt Romney." www.time.com

As a consequence of their belief there are numerous anti-Trump marches and protests. A few individuals even engage in violence and have to be arrested. The USA Democracy believes in the citizenry's right to protest and thus permits protests even if there is no true reason for one in the face of the known and published facts.

The Congress of the USA refuses to cooperate with the Presidency fully. In fact there are those who are talking about impeaching President Trump and are actively seeking evidence to carry out their intention. There are those in the Republican Party who refuse to accept President Trump's leadership in spite of the fact that Mr. Trump ran as a Republican against the Democrat, Hilary Clinton. There are those who believed that Hilary Clinton would have won, and, because of their belief, they refuse to accept that Mr. Trump is now President Trump. Because one believes it to be so does not make it so. So what is the use or value of "believing?"

There are those millions of people who believe that she/he will win the lottery. As a result of this erroneous belief millions of people buy millions of dollars worth of lottery tickets but only one (from the millions) will actually win. What are the statistical chances of an individual winning the lottery? "There are 22,957,480 different ways in which 6 numbers can be chosen from a total of 53 numbers. Therefore, the odds of correctly choosing the winning combination is 1 to 22,957,480." www.floridalottery.com. Now we know what the odds are would we stop playing by not buying lottery tickets?

What is the point of knowing when, having known, one does not change one's behavior? We see accidents on the roads and highways. However, most of us believe that we will not be involved in an accident. Is it trues that because I believe that I will not be involved in an accident that I will truly not be involved in one? Is it true that because I believe that I will win the lottery that I will win the lottery? Is it true that because I believe that Hilary Clinton will win the presidential election in the USA that she will actually win? Is it true that because I believe that the earth is flat and not round that the earth is truly flat and not round? Is it true that because I believe that rats are the cause of the Plague and not the insanitary conditions that this, my belief, makes the rats the culprit?

Our individual and collective beliefs hold back our personal and collective growth and development. But, let's be ware, for, knowledge is a burdensome thing.

There are so many people who continue to believe (and say) that OJ Simpson is guilty of murder in spite of the fact that he was found ***not guilty*** in a court of law under the public's scrutiny and the ever-present media.

People continue to believe that it was all a hoax about a man landing on the moon – that no man ever landed on the moon. They believe that it was all a staged and fabricated incident not unlike the making of movies. How about commercials? Are they true? Yet millions of people are influenced by them to make purchases of "stuff" they do not need or want. Beliefs influence behaviors. Why do people do what they do, especially what they do with respect to their religion? Poor, old females, in particular, give their last penny to the wealthy church! This is the power of belief: it makes people irrational and causes them do what is unreasonable, even if it is to their personal disadvantage or demise.

We are programmed and/or forced by the elite status quo to all have the same beliefs; lining us up like cloned rubber-duckies. Yet the few who dared and think outside the box or question any of the principles, tenets, carved-in-stone beliefs of the established status quo are, sooner or later, crucified for doing so. So, why take the risk of thinking outside the box?

A few cannot help it even though they are fully aware that they are risking their lives in doing so. However, society cannot move forward without questioning and the testing of old ideas, which results in the creation of new ideas.

HOW EQUAL ARE WE? Essay #10

"The quotation 'All men are created equal' has been called an 'immortal declaration,' and 'perhaps [the] single phrase' of the American Revolutionary period with the greatest 'continuing importance.[1][2] *Thomas Jefferson first used the phrase in the U.S. Declaration of Independence, which he penned in 1776 during the beginning of the American Revolution. It was thereafter quoted and incorporated into speeches by a wide array of substantial figures in American political and social life in the United States. The final form of the phrase was stylized by Benjamin Franklin.*[3]*"* <u>www.wikipedia.org</u>

Before President Trump became President Trump, he was Mr. Trump, a private citizen and businessman. Who can argue that Mr. Trump was treated much differently from how he is currently being treated as President Trump? During the week of May 20th 2017 President Trump and his wife was on an official tour of the Middle East, Israel, Palestine, Italy and Brussels. They received many unique and expensive gifts! Would they have received these lavish gifts if they were not the highest US government officials? In any event as citizen Trump and businessman, the couple is reported to be among the rich elite of the world. Is citizen Trump treated the same way as a poor American citizen of no financial worth is treated? How equal are we?

Do the American Police treat all American citizens equally? There are thousands of cases of discrimination by all levels of Police – local, state, and federal. "The Equal Employment Opportunity Commission (EEOC) will not go out of business. Charges of racial discrimination and sexual harassment have increased every single decade since Title VII was passed in 1964. The statistics are chilling:

- Sexual harassment charges increased 146 percent between 1992 and 2001.
- They have increased150, 000 percent since 1980. (1)
- Pregnancy discrimination charges increased 126 percent between 1992 and 2001. (2)
- Sexual discrimination charges increased 112 percent during the same period. (3)
- Racial discrimination charges increased 484 percent between the 1980-1989 decade and the 1990-1999 decade. (4)
- National origin charges increased 112 percent in the period 1992-2001. (5)

What's worse is that the above numbers account for only some of the discrimination suits that have been filed. Not all complaints go through the EEOC; some are filed independently." An article by *Jennifer Hicks* in www.imdiversity.com

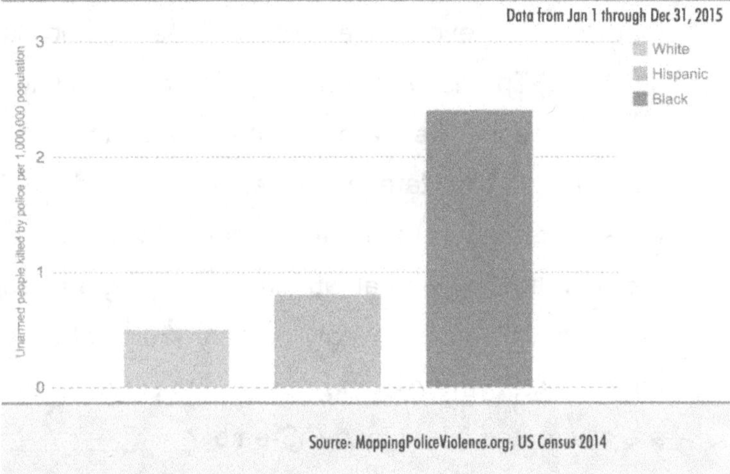

The federal government as well as non-governmental organizations are monitoring and mapping the numerical and locational occurrences of discrimination, unfair treatment, by the Police to the general population and by race/ethnicity. So, there can be no doubt that civil and criminal illegal discrimination occurs through out the USA. How can this documented illegal discrimination be reconciled with the proclamation that "all men are created equal?" Why do people continue to espouse that there is equality in the USA when the evidence, both anecdotal and statistical, deny this preached falsity? Are we delusionary?

The perpetuation of this falsity that "all men are created equal" is further burdensome when we become aware that "one in every five persons" has some kind of disability. This is pertinent here since it is stated that, even though we are treated unequally by the government, the state, and local officials, and the Police, we are created equal by the Creator. When some of us are born healthy with all our limbs, senses, and dormant faculties while some twenty percent (20%) of us are not so fortunate, where is the truth in the statement that we are all created equal by our Creator?

In a classroom of 25 students with the same teacher, the same learning tools and supplies, the same learning environment, the same school administration, etc. do they all learn or achieve equally? We all know that the answer to this question is "No." How can it be claimed that we are all created equal by our Creator?

Perhaps we will be better served if we are willing to allow ourselves to accept the reality that we are not created equal, not even by our Creator. Who is equal to the Pope? The words of Shakespeare come to mind: "some are born great; some achieve greatness; and some have greatness entrusted upon them." This comes closer to accurately describing our reality and should be enough for our understanding of our world rather than for us to pursue the unattainable theoretical rhetoric that "all men are created equal."

When a millionaire can buy a dinner for himself at a cost of over $100 and then throw it away because he does not like it but a child, born in the home of a poor woman, cannot have money to even buy a packet of biscuits; when holiday makers can have unlimited gasoline to enjoy themselves in various water sports, producing nothing, while farmers cannot afford to purchase gasoline to operate farm machinery in many parts of the world to produce food, how can this notion that all men are created equal be true?

When 90% of the wealth created in the USA is owned and controlled by one tenth of one percent (.01%) of the population; when one individual has more money than some countries, where is the equality of all men? When you are OK and I am not OK; or, when I am OK and you are not OK, how can we be equal? When one man, or one woman, has access to several sex partners while another has none, where is the truth in this inherently falsely acclaimed statement that all men are created equal? When one man, or one woman, has three jobs while another has none, we cannot be equal. Must we learn to accept this inequality as the natural order of life, that it is ordained by the Creator?

When the United States of America became a nation in 1776 there was specific help from Russia and France. Perhaps the nation and state of the USA might not have become a reality without the help that was received from these two countries. China and India were not contending economies or states at that time. There was, at that time, a totally different political reality. England was the enemy of the new nation and did all that it could to see to it that the USA would be a short-lived democracy.

The Founding Fathers of the USA (God bless their souls) designed a Constitution embodying the concept of *"separation of powers."* This gave us a bicameral law-making body: the House of Representatives and the Senate; the Presidency with executive authority; and the Judicial branch with authority to adjudicate in accordance with their interpretation of the laws made by the law-making body, the Congress. There were to be no king or queen, as it was in England at the time, who had absolute authority. (But "trice did Caesar refuse the crown." Is it only the symbolic crown that makes the king a king? Or is the powers conferred upon him because of the office he holds and the powers he assumes, especially in the advent of war?)

The reality today in the USA is a constant intra and inter fighting between and among the three branches of the Government of the USA. The House of Representative is at odds with the Senate. (They debate and debate and debate! They have "hearings" and hearings" but quickly go back to their old, established way of conducting the affairs of Government.) The Congress refuses to work with the Presidency. (It is obvious that they see that their purpose is to object to and interrupt the agenda of the elected President who has acquired the powers inherent in the Presidency.) The Judiciary is ready to deny the President's executive orders with which he is forced to govern because the Congress refuses to pass appropriate laws to give him the moral, legal and financial authority to govern affectively and effectively. Is it this infighting that the Founding Fathers expected or wanted? Well, they designed the Constitution of the USA!

The seating arrangement in the Congress is visible evidence of the division in the governance of the USA. The individuals who were elected on a Democrat ticket sit on one side while the those who were elected on a

Republican ticket sit on the other side, each ready to oppose the other just to oppose, even though there is no reason to oppose. Many a time there is opposition just because the individual who introduces a bill may not have the seniority or because the core clique does not like him/her. The needs of the USA are of no importance to them and are given no consideration. (The seating arrangement in the houses of Congress must be rearranged. Members of Congress should sit in alphabetical order by state: Alaska, Arizona, Arkansas, etc., without any division.) Again, the infighting continues with each state fighting for itself (NY and California, for example)

There is no doubt that this constant inter and intra fighting between and among the three branches of government of the USA is rendering the governance of the USA weak, slow and ineffective. How often have we not heard the phrase *"lame duck Congress?"* The Congress is dysfunctional, to say the least.

Russia and China, on the other hand, do not have a Constitution that is designed by their Founding Fathers that incorporates the concept of "separation of powers." They have a Parliament with parliamentarians elected by the people, the electorate. One people, one country, one

Parliament! They are clearly benefiting from the inherent efficiency of this "one party" system. Why do we need two, three, four (and, in some cases, many) political parties in one and the same country? This is waste at the highest level!

Russia and China have become rivals of the USA in about a century. This has happened because there is a significant reduction in time and resources wasted in debate and hearings as in the USA. Russia has successfully sent the first human in space before the USA. Russia is challenging the USA in political and international relations. China is almost neck-to-neck with the USA in size and quantity of its economy. And, China has done this in half the time it took the USA to develop its economy to what it is today. It is a fact that the economy of Russia and China developed at a faster rate than the USA.

If China and Russia, with their "one party" governance systems, were to cooperate or join forces, the USA will become a sore looser soon.

Even if they do not join forces, we can expect the USA to continue to loose in the world's political, economic and military arenas. The three competing branches of government will ensure that this will happen because it is an inefficient design. It was a reaction to the then British system and is not a fully thought out and thought through system. The Russian and Chinese systems are a reaction to the system of the USA, and, as such have gone one step better, just as how the USA's system went one step better than the British system at that time.

The Founding Fathers of the USA's system did say that the Constitution is a "living document," meaning that it can be changed. But it hasn't been changed since its adoption in 1788. The designs of cars have changed; the designs of houses have changed; fashion has changed; the design of roads and railways have changed, etc. but the "living" Constitution of the USA has not been changed to make it more efficient.

India now has the "fastest growing" economy. So, currently, the USA must contend with Russia in the political and military arenas; with China in the economic and political arena; and, very soon, with India in the economic arena. Even though India has a two-party corrupt system, India is making great strides in the economic arena. What if India were to change to a one-India, one-party system, like China and Russia, what would this mean for the USA?

The USA is already loosing to China in the rate of economic development and it will soon loose to India in the rate of economic development while it is loosing to Russia in international and political relations. All this is happening while the three branches of government of the USA, as is now more than evident, it is obvious, with the Presidency of Donald J. Trump, constantly fighting among them selves, each for supremacy over the other! If the USA is to remain competitive in the current economic, political and military realities, it must reform its two and a half century old Constitution. This constitutes the most important battle for the USA. Does the USA have the political will to accomplish this? Can we achieve this when we are always "looking back" and fighting among ourselves? Now the states (with sanctuary cities) are challenging the authority of the federal government under the Presidency of Donald J. Trump.

These debilitating practices and inherent weakness of the Government of the USA (because of the design of its Constitution, which incorporates the concept of "separation of powers") make it very easy for Vladimir Putin of Russia and Xi Jinping of China to overcome and surpass the influence and privilege the USA enjoyed in the past. There is a new world order and the USA will not be the dominating nation as it used to be. The aging and divisive Constitution of the USA will see to this.

The passenger jet touched down at JFK International Airport with a bump and a screech. The lights all around were dazzling and this made legal immigrant Mr. R. N. Hope, with his slightly plush goatee, rather confused. He had never seen so much electric light in his entire thirty-three years of living in Guyana. He was worried stiff. Would someone be at the airport to "receive" him? What if no one was there? All the money he had on him was US$200 in a visa money order. He had an address. But, if she was not there to receive him at the airport, why go to her address? Would she accept him? It was nearly two years since they saw each other. She went to Guyana to marry him. They had a brief personal and sexual encounter and she left for the USA. I guess she was "checking" him out – his sexual ability and stamina. Who can say with any certainty? Only she knows why she did what she did.

The unseaworthy wooden bateau was hesitant, as if it had a mind of its own, as if it had pre-knowledge of the impending dangers that will befall the hapless illegal immigrants who sat nervously on the gunwales anxiously awaiting their departure from Haiti. Monsieur Olivier Fears had paid the boat captain the US$500 that the captain demanded to take him to Florida and put him ashore somewhere along the Atlantic seacoast. "What was the delay?" he wondered. Haiti had become unbearable for him since he spoke his mind about the new President of Haiti and his opinion was published in the local paper. They were after his blood; he had to get out, and very soon.

He took all the money they had saved up, he and his wife, and paid the captain. What was the delay? The captain was nowhere to be seen and each passenger was afraid of the other, afraid that one would tell on the other. He was afraid that the ton ton macoute would appear from the dark shadows of the moonless Caribbean night and grab him and kill him and no one would ever say a word or care. As if in his dream he heard a quick stutter in creole. It was the captain's voice. "There is a storm," said the cold empty voice, coming from somewhere in the front of the now rapidly rolling open-top boat. "This is not good," Olivier mused. But, actually, he murmured, without his knowing it.

No one spoke. The silence was beginning to bear down upon his shoulders like a ton of lead and he shrugged involuntarily to shake it off. But it remained with him and now his mind was threatening to separate from him, to leave him stranded, but ashore. In his mind he was already somewhere near Miami, on land, in the USA, making his way to a main road. Ah, road and road and paved road with no holes; the roads are so smooth and wide. All the cars in Haiti can fit on them at one and the same time and there will still be room for more and more and more. "I will buy myself a nice car," he said to himself. "What it must be to be a citizen of the USA!" he said softly, as softly as the cool North East Trade winds that gently touched the rough black skin of his face, skin that was made rough from constantly shaving with the same razor blades that could not cut even butter in the hot Caribbean sun.

Mr. R. N. Hope had his large yellowish brown envelope in his hand. He was ready to take his place in the New York medley as a legal immigrant. He had his visa in the envelope. So he was told by the Consular Officer at the embassy of the United States of America in Kingston, Georgetown, Guyana.

The Immigration Officer at JFK International, terminal four (4), looked over R.N. Hope scrupulously. It seemed as if he was making up his mind about something. "Surely, everything must be all right," R.N. thought. "I did not buy this visa, like so many others. Visas are for sale in Guyana. You just have to have the right connection and can hang out at Tower or the Pegasus hotels. You know, you have to have money. Money buys everything, not good character or good deeds."

"Welcome," said the Immigration Officer. Mr. R.N. Hope heard but did not understand.

"You mean no bribe! In Guyana one has to bribe to get anything done. Bribery and corruption and discrimination is the norm," he reflected.

"Welcome," the spectacularly uniformed white Immigration Officer repeated. "This way out. Show the customs form to the Customs Officer on your way out."

"This is not what Jagan and the comrades of his political party, the PPP, reported about "'Americans,'" mused R.N. Hope to himself. They were vehement in their assertions that the problems Guyanese are experiencing are all due to "American Imperialism" and "Capitalism." According to Jagan and his PPP comrades the only viable solution for Guyana is "communism!" Jagan declared that he is a "Communist" and that white Americans are racist and not to be trusted. Yet he visits the USA time and time again to be the beneficiary of hundreds of thousands (if not millions) of US dollars for his communist political party. How ironical! The very set of Guyanese, especially Indo-Guyanese, who fled Guyana to escape him, his communism, and Burnham, his socialism and racism, generously gave him their hard-earned US dollars, earned after going to work in snow and sleet and ice year after year.

There was only one way out to exit to the international arrivals hall, and so, even though R.N. Hope was actively contemplating turning back, he couldn't. One small but reluctant step by one small but reluctant step he gingered forward, clutching onto his brief case. "Am I in the right place?" he argued with himself. "This must be the place. Everyone who was at the immigration counters is here." And, "look at people, people of every kind, shape and size!"

"R.N." he heard a strange voice calling out. "Your wife sent us for you. This way man, this way. Here countryman put on this jacket and scarf. It is still cold outside."

"This can't be true," thought R.N. But then, recognizing one of them, he said to himself: "Oh yes! Yes! I think I remember that young fella. He is her last brother. Yes! Yes! It is he," R.N. silently concluded. "Hey fellas. I am R.N," he hailed out to the group of three men whom he thought looked like Guyanese.

Any way they had his name written on a piece of paper, which they displayed.

Even in his distress Olivier began to feel sleepy. The choppy and violently crashing waves were now weak and slow and were gently rocking the boat and the swaying was encouraging his drowsiness. He hadn't slept in days and nights because of his anxiety. His imagination and fears would not let him rest. "Sleep," what was that?

He did not even touch his wife for weeks even though he considered her very attractive and most desirable. "No sex," he cautioned himself, because her sweet moanings and enticing murmurs would have kept him cemented, like a statue, to Haiti and his certain murder. "Truth!" "'Truth,' they say, 'will set you free.'" "I spoke the truth but this is what I got," he thought. "I should have kept my mouth shut, like everyone else, and I would not have had to leave like this, risking my life and sure to loose my wife."

"Don't fall asleep, Olivier. You will fall over board and you will never make it to Miami. I guarantee you that. If you don't believe me, try it and you will see," the captain murmured as he passed by Olivier on his way to the stern of the boat. "We are leaving now. Satay awake if you wish to arrive in the USA. I know you know 'swimology,' but you must stay awake!" It sounded like an order and Olivier was unaccustomed to being ordered but he claimed to have a "democratic, open mind," and "this was no time to argue, not with the captain, the only man who could help him."

"Anyway…anyway, this is the captain," Olivier counseled himself. "I have to go to America and this is my only way to get there. I cannot leave by plane. They will catch me like a stray dog at the airport and take me straight back to my home or murder me in some backwoods and dump my body in the street." These thoughts woke him up and kept him awake. Then, in a moment, some men in silhouette pushed the boat out to sea. They were off to the USA at last, the land of "freedom and opportunity."

The wind was brisk and the sea was rough most of the time. Well, that was what Olivier thought. This was his first time out in the open Atlantic. All he knew was the shore waters of the leeward side of Haiti where he used to swim almost daily. And, any way, the sun was coming up. He guessed that they were way off of Haiti and out of the reach of the President's death squads. So, at least, that was one thing he did not have to worry about. Or, so he thought.

As if reading his thoughts and responding to what he was thinking, the captain said flatly: "no one is free yet. The military sea patrol can show up at any time. And, after them, there is the American Coast Guard who is constantly on the look out for boats from Haiti. We can all be locked up in America and then sent right back. We are not treated like the Cubans are treated. We are poor, black Haitians."

The sun was bright and hot. Olivier wondered where any one could hide in bright sunshine from the military sea patrol or from the American Coast Guard. There was drinking water on the boat. So, he went to get a sip. He, like the tens of others on the overloaded boat, knew quite well that water is the most precious commodity in the Oceans – drinking water. There was water all around you. But, if you are thirsty, and you drink the salty seawater, you will become thirstier. And, drinking more and more of the salty seawater is sure to kill you. "A sip, only a sip," he thought, even though he felt like gulping down half the plastic jimmy john. "Where could one hide," he kept thinking.

Mr. R.N. Hope donned the light jacket and wrapped the scarf around his neck. He immediately felt the difference in temperature as he stepped out of the terminal building and hurried with his associates to a huge parking lot where there were thousands of cars. He had never before seen so many cars in one place. The fellas tried to speak with him, asking him about the plane trip and Guyana. He wasn't sure what to say. In fact, in the plane, his uncertainty had enveloped him and so he did not have the presence of mind to "enjoy the flight" as the airhostess suggested. "What is there to 'enjoy' on a flight anyway and why do they all say these words?" he queried in his mind.

The car wound around here and there in a most unpredictable route, (unpredictable to R.N.), and eventually stopped in front of a house. R.N. had no idea where he was or by what route he arrived at that location. What he took notice of, however, was the unending number of cars lining both sides of the street. He thought that there must be a wedding in the neighborhood. This is the only time so many cars are to be seen lining the street, as far as he knew. He went inside the house where he met the woman whom he married some two years ago. It was not a romantic meeting or a romantic reunion.

Olivier Fears either lost consciousness from exhaustion or fell asleep briefly. He regained his perception suddenly when the boat began to roll and shake as the size and rapidity of the waves increased. The white of the bulging eyes of his fellow escapees were getting bigger and bigger as a storm began to brew in earnest. Would this be the end for him and his fellow escapees? Or would the Lord spare them all to get to the shore somewhere in Florida. Anywhere would be fine with him, so long as he arrived somewhere in America. They all began to pray, forgetting most of their other predicaments. At least, that was what he thought.

He turned his head to take a look at the captain. The captain was holding on firmly to the naked wooden arm of the rudder as the sails bulged under the pressure of the winds of the approaching storm. Somehow the resolute and composed look on the captain's face gave him some respite from his multiple sources of fears and anxiety. After all, the captain made this trip many times before. The army sea patrol or the American Coast Guard never picked him up. Olivier had heard by word of mouth from his many acquaintances and friends in Haiti that this captain is the best and, so, is his best chance of ever getting to America. So he paid the price and took his chances with him. He was stuck with him now!

Somehow and without any fancy compass or other navigation instruments the captain successfully piloted his rickety-looking craft back and forth from Haiti to Florida. As his mind became absorbed with these reassuring thoughts, Olivier noticed that the sails were no longer bulging with the pressure of the wind of a storm. They appeared to look more normal and the rocking and rolling of the boat was getting less and less. It appeared that the captain was skillfully able to steer them away from the threatening storm or that the impending storm simply missed them because they were not directly in its path. Many of his fellow passengers said that the Lord answered their prayers and showed His mercy unto them.

Olivier Fears thought about taking out the book he had brought with him to read as the boat steadied and made progress towards the USA. After some hesitation he retrieved the book about Toussaint Louverture and his bringing of the ideas of Democracy to Haiti and the Western hemisphere. The book absorbed him beyond his belief as he read and dozed off and read and dozed off while the boat journeyed on to America where, he believed, democracy was the order of the day. When would he arrive in America?

Ms. Frances Flores woke up late as usual. She looked about her as if to make sure she knew where she was and that she was not still in her dream world. The room looked familiar. It was a mess. Her clothes were scattered here and there and there and here. All kinds of wrappings and small boxes were piled up on the bed she fell asleep on. As she became aware of her surroundings and her feelings, she also realized that she was trembling slightly. She felt an intense emptiness inside of her as she tried to sit up on the bed. She looked at the clock that was hanging loosely on the opposite wall. It was almost 4.00 p.m. Her supplier and savior would be here soon. She got up.

Frances was born in Brooklyn, New York. She was a U.S. citizen by birth. She did not have to get any "green card." She was born free, as free as the wind blows, in the land of the free and the home of the brave. Frances knew that she was addicted to drugs. Her habit started with prescription drugs. The doctor had prescribed a series of opiate drugs for her headache and depression.

She got dressed, made herself a cup of coffee and tried to eat some dry cereal directly from the box. Leaving her mess on the countertop, she went outside.

The small park was about a quarter of a mile away. She walked directly to the park and sat down on the old wooden bench in the park. She kept looking about and around her. Apparently she was scouting for the presence of any police car. Satisfied that there was none, she stood up and yelled, "yo, yo, yo!" and sat herself back down. An old woman who was trudging along on the street, pushing an overloaded handcart entered the park and sat next to Frances. She looked Frances over, sizing her up.

"I am very hungry," said the old woman loudly. "Can you give me some money so that I can buy me a something to eat?"

Without any hesitation, like a Good Samaritan, Frances placed some folded-up money in the old woman's outstretched hand. The old woman gathered herself, pushing her cart in front of her, and exited the park. Directly next to Frances remained a small paper bag as if it was hers and it had been there all the time. Frances did not attempt to pick up the paper bag but remained seated next to it. She kept looking around as if she was expecting some one else. Then she picked up the paper bag and casually sauntered out of the park, making her way back to her house. She had collected her drug supply for another week for yet more fixes! "I'm alright now," she assured herself. Upon arriving home, she went directly to her bedroom and "did her thing." The euphoria soon gripped her and she collapsed on he bed.

R.N. hope received his "green card," got a job, worked briefly and saved up some money. Since he had applied for acceptance in the university of Minnesota while he was in Guyana, he left New York to attend university in the state of Minnesota.

The captain said, "Olivier, Oliver! Jump overboard and swim towards that light to the right. That's Florida. The Coat Guard is coming. I can hear the sound of their boat. I am sure it's them." Olivier did not move. He did not comprehend anything.

"Jump over board and swim to Florida? Did he hear right?" queried Olivier to himself in disbelief.

"Olivier, Olivier, you must do it now or else you will be locked up like the rest of us. You are strong and healthy, man. Swim for your freedom. Many have done it before. Jump now!" screamed the captain.

Olivier jumped, purely because of the insistence of the captain's voice and the sound of the boat he could have then heard. In the water he soon realized that the current was an ally and all he had to do was to stay afloat and guide himself towards the light. "That light is the light of freedom," he thought as he got control of himself and started to swim earnestly but slowly in the cooling water.

After about an hour of real time, but an eternity to Olivier ("there are many days in a minute"), he spied a portion of a floating tree trunk. He swam towards it and put his right arm over and around it. He floated and drifted along with the log towards what must be the shore, he thought. Anyway, the short log provided an opportunity for him to rest and get his breathing under control. He did not want to get too tired; in fact he couldn't get too tired.

Without his anticipation Olivier realized that his feet were touching land! He was able to stand upright with his nose above water. He tried to stand, not really convinced and still doubtful, with his hand firmly on the log. He breathed deeply as he convinced himself that his feet were on firm land. Still holding on to the floating log he walked towards the shoreline with some trepidation still. He was now in America! He felt like screaming to high heaven but he reluctantly restrained himself from doing so for he quickly realized that it was dangerous and unwise.

Mr. R.N. Hope completed his graduate degree, became a program manager at a New York non-profit, and, according to a Haitian female associate's prediction, became a "biggie" in the NYC Indo-Caribbean community. As a program manager, instructor and counselor, Mr. R. N. Hope, now Prof. R.N. Hope, trained tens of thousands of New Yorkers who were welfare recipients and drug abusers, elevating them from the lowest rounds of American society, and made them productive, tax-paying members of society.

He paid all taxes due. He made his contributions to Medicare and Social Security, and, while a member of the faculty of a community college, was forced to be a member of the faculty union, (union rules). He made contributions to a retirement plan designed by "financial experts" and sold to the faculty union members in collusion with the Union. When he signed up for and began paying in to his Social Security Account, he was informed that he will receive Social Security benefits at age 65, like millions of other citizens all over the United States of America.

At a point in his life, R.N. Hope became an American citizen. So, as a citizen, he can vote in national elections, and become a participating and contributing citizen of the United States of America, heart and soul. According to R.N. he was as "American as apple pie." (Apple pie became a favorite desert of his)

Monsieur Olivier Fears from Haiti, having arrived in the USA by boat, (an illegal immigrant) eventually made his way to Brooklyn, New York. There is a thriving Haitian community in the Flat Bush area of Brooklyn, NY. And, so, it was only natural for him to have gravitated to live among his "own" group. He worked three jobs sometimes, when he was able to find work. He saved his money to buy that car he dreamed about.

The difference was that, even though he bought a car, it was not only a car; it was a taxicab. He bought a yellow cab medallion from NYC. He paid cash for this prized and coveted investment. Olivier also became a citizen of the U. S. of A. at some point.

As a self-employed taxicab owner and operator he soon acquired some savings. He paid his taxes, his Social Security and Medicare contributions, regularly and on time. This is what it means to be an "American," according to him.

Now both R.N. Hope and Olivier Fears are retired. They are both citizens of the United States by naturalization. One arrived legally by jet and the other illegally by boat.

Frances Flores, a born US citizen, who never worked for any continuous period in her life, but benefited from all the welfare programs on behalf of herself and her children, is also now "retired" because of her age and is entitled to all benefits and entitlements available to US citizens. She has a taxpayer paid social worker whose legal responsibility it is to ensure that Frances receives all the benefits she is entitled to, including "food stamps" and housing. These are called entitlements. She is entitled to them even though she never paid a dime in taxes, or made any contribution to Social Security or Medicare. She receives Medicaid, a health insurance program paid for by the state and federal governments of the USA from tax dollars collected by the state and federal governments from working citizens and legal residents of the USA.

R.N. Hope and Olivier cannot benefit from any entitlements since their financial situations exclude them from entitlements. Their savings and Social Security benefits, their previous contributions, now prevent them from receiving any food stamps or housing assistance. Even though both of them made separate (separate from the taxes they paid) contributions to Medicare, they have to yet pay for Medicare-based health insurance coverage. Frances, on the other hand, has a taxpayer paid social worker working within the government's bureaucracy and multitude of laws to ensure that she receives all her entitlements, including Medicaid.

Why become a citizen of the United States of America? No wonder so many illegal immigrants prefer to remain illegal and work "off the books" and send the bulk of their earnings back to their home countries, including Mexico. In the mean while these illegals usually are "entitled" to free medical services, the legal protection of the Courts (even against tax-paying citizens of the USA) and other benefits.   Mr. and Ms. Citizens get their paid-up and paid-in benefits reduced or denied by the very US government that collected taxes from them for decades, noting, also, that their contributions to Medicare and Social Security are NOT taxes. And, thus, the US government does not have a unilateral right to make decisions to reduce or deny citizens receiving what they saved up for their retirement while those who never paid any income tax or made any contribution to any government retirement savings plan are "entitled" to certain and specific benefits and get they them.

Victur Victorius, a Vietnam veteran, of Chicago, Illinois hitch hiked his way to NYC. He had no money to pay the Greyhound fare. To him NYC is a haven for begging, especially for veterans. So, like flowers that are attractive to honeybees, NYC is a magnet for Victur, especially during the summer months when millions of tourists swarm onto NYC. Begging became his "profession" soon after he was discharged from the army after the Vietnam War was brought to an end by the advocacy of the hippie generation. Victur, of course, returned home from Vietnam to find "his" wife with her third boyfriend. "No war, no money, no wife…no life!" so reasoned Victur with whatever reasoning abilities he had left after the killings and murders in 'Nam.

Victur had left his wife and two children back in Chicago to enlist in the US army to go to Vietnam to kill communist Vietcongs by the hundreds or thousands. Enlisting was quick and easy and the pay was great! So, why not enlist, especially since he was unable to find a good-paying job for many months? As a Black American he is the last to be hired but as a Black American he was sure he would be the first to be enlisted into military service at that time.

He and his fellow servicemen fought in Vietnam to defend and protect Americans – millions of American, with money in their pockets, who ride the NYC subway daily to and from work. Victur had decided that this captured audience will be his source of meager sustenance. "Why not?" he asked himself. "After all, it is they he risked his life for. While they were at home in the US of A, enjoying themselves, he was busting his behind in the swamps of Vietnam, fighting the Vietcongs." If he had a conscience, this was his way of rationalizing his behavior as a beggar because he considered himself a Vietnam War victim. He strongly believed that his fellow Americans owed him something and, thus, he had no qualms about asking them to help him out now that he was down and out.

Victur arrived in NYC late that evening. He went to "work" immediately in the subway station at 42nd Street. After about an hour he collected almost $12. He could get a sandwich, something to drink and buy a subway token. With a token he can enter the subway system and change from train to train, giving himself a larger and wider captive audience. He would be able to increase his chances as a Vietnam veteran beggar!

Victur slept on a platform bench that night. He was tired after a very active day. At about 7:00 a.m. he woke up and got up. There were a few would-be passengers waiting on the platform. "Hey Sir, can you tell me the time?" he hailed out to a would-be passenger who was well attired in a well-fitting suit.

The man said: "it is exactly 7:00 a.m." without looking at him.

"Thank you, sir," replied Victur. "I am a Vietnam veteran and I am homeless. I fought to defend America's interest and people like you. Can you spare me a dollar for coffee? I do need something to eat; I didn't have anything to eat since yesterday when I arrived from Chicago. Can you help me out?" Victur stated his case flatly and sounded as though he wasn't speaking to any one in particular.

"You are a Vietnam veteran?" queried the man. "Why not go to the V.A.?" the man wanted to know.

"The V.A.?" rejoined Victur in disgust. "Those people are only interested in themselves and the rules they made to deny us veterans any descent service and care. How many billions go to the V.A. and how much of that do we veterans get?"

The man said nothing in reply. He just stood there as if he did not hear any one and as if he hadn't said anything. It was as if Victur no longer existed. His train arrived. He entered it and Victur ceased to exist, not even in his memory, perhaps.

Why should he be bothered? The federal government should take care of the veterans and not have them molest the innocent public. After all US taxpayers pay trillions in taxes and billions are allocated for "Veterans' Affairs!" This is how the government of the USA treats the veterans and citizens of the USA. Why become a citizen and, worse yet, why enlist in the service to fight for the USA when there are thousands of veterans, like Victur, who are homeless and hungry while the V.A. staff and officials are living the good and prosperous life? Who is "Mr. and Ms. US citizen?"

The intercontinental jet taxies on the apron and makes its way to Gate No. 13. at Orlando International Airport (OIA – MCO). The brightly written name on the jet liner says "Emirates" in English and Arabic.

After some time a woman dressed in the Muslim Hijab dress and accompanied by four children approached the US immigration officer's console. She had a large yellowish brown envelope in her hand. This is the usual package in which the immigration papers are placed for travel to the USA. She is a legal immigrant.

The only difference between her and R.N. Hope is that she and her four children are classified as refugees.

As refugees they are immediately entitled to all the rights and benefits of US citizens who have paid taxes for the major part of their lives, who have made contributions to Social Security and Medicare, and who have voted in the Presidential election to elect President Barak Obama. President Obama authorized the refugee program. According to him we (who is the we?) have agreed to accept some 1,500 refugees. But, according to President Trump, we have already accepted over 50,000 refugees. Which number is the correct number?

Whatever the number is, these refugees are brought here on international jet liners and are immediately given housing, food stamp, Medicaid, and cash allowances and a path to citizenship, they and their children! Legal immigrants like R.N. Hope have to start from zero with zero.

Olivier Fears, R.N. Hope, veteran Victur Victurious, and millions of other US citizens make inhuman sacrifices in the USA and on the battlefields to make this nation what it is. The refugees from oil super rich monarchies arrive in luxury and style and are immediately entitled to all rights, benefits and privileges, and immediately become equals of US citizens!

This is what the government of the USA has put into place for folks who have made no contribution to the USA and the American way of life. The Congress, the Presidency and the Judiciary are advocates for non-US citizens while veterans and builders of the American society and contributors to the American way of life are having their Social Security benefits reduced and or denied and are not eligible for Medicaid if they own a home. Veterans sleep in the NYC subway, are forced to become beggars and molest the public "for something to eat" wile newly arrived refugees are brought here on luxury jet liners as equals with rights and entitlements.

When they were making their millions from the "black gold" in their home countries, did they ever offer (or send) any to any US citizen? Why must US citizens who have paid the price in sacrifice and money to become US citizens foot the bill for ten of thousands of freeloaders who are labeled "refugees?" Are there any incentive or benefits for becoming a citizen of the USA – to become Mr. and Ms. US Citizen?

"INDENTURESHIP" Essay #13

Why the profusion of "scholarly" articles about Identureship? What is to be "proven?" And, if anything is to be "proven," what constitutes "proof?" Who requires proof? And, who is proving what to whom and with whose "facts?"

So they write books, now they can write. And some of them hire Cooks, claiming they are so bright! Yet, they are oppressed.

*And some are even possessed by spirits of Dutch and such as they Use religion as a crutch! And some of them are very rich but soon Become a "son-of-a-*itch!"*

Never mind how dressed they may be: their minds are in the gutter - See? Ah! They write books - These intellectual crooks!

What good are their books if only for how the cover looks? Who Cares of their claim? But now some have fame and a few have a Known "name" While their oppression remains the same!

They mimic their masters like dogs and gangsters proudly called doctors as they join their oppressors.

They write books - these intellectual crooks!

Indentureship was a fact. It happened. After the abolition of slavery: the European colonists had an imminent need for able labor. What is wrong with importing labor under contract? We still import labor under contract today. And, up until today, some contractual laborers choose to remain in the countries into which they have been imported. And they soon settle in the host countries and become contributing members of their host societies even as they hold on to their traditions with tenacity.

Movement of population around the globe, over time, is absolutely necessary for the mixing of the genetic pool. Inbreeding fosters disease and deformity.

With the establishment of political boundaries (forming countries) natural movement of population is impeded and/or controlled. The demand for laborers, then and now, in the context of these political controls, necessitates, then and now, some other "legal" means to allow for a "free" movement of population, especially workers, world-wide.

The colonists came up with the "legal scheme" of contractual labor – Identureship. Labor was, and still is, a legalized, trade-able commodity.

Would the Indians have voluntarily left India for the West Indies? Some recruitment was necessary. We still recruit workers today. Successful recruitment requires some type of incentive and false advertising, as is noticeable up to now.

When an employer recruits and hires laborers, is the employer responsible for the living conditions and social cohesion of the hired hands?

The Identureship system was legally different from Slavery in that the recruited indentured laborers signed contracts to work for a specified period of time for wages. They were paid for their labor. And, the British colonists, by contract, established and contributed to a remigration fund to repatriate those who, having completed their term of idnetureship, were free to return to India, passage prepaid. Slavery did not bequeath these legal luxuries to the enslaved.

In spite of these legal guarantees many writers from the Indian and Afro diaspora are quick to claim similarities between the systems of Slavery and Identureship. There are no legal or operational similarities.

One hundred years later more people of Indian origin speak and write English – more than the born British! Of course, there are those folks who are people of Indian origin (PIOs) and non-resident Indians (NRIs) who are more "British" than folks who are born of direct British stock!

There are those who excite themselves with the notion

that Indenturehip, as conceived and practiced by the British, was solely for the profit and benefit of the plantation owners such as Booker and Sambach Parker (in Guiana) and that the Identured (contracted) laborers were exploited beyond what is humanly possible. But the observable economic realities belie, and disallow, this begrudging notion. Those contract-laborers, who chose to remain in the colonies, own (***but do not control***) significant wealth in the now "independent" colonies. A useful comparison can be made by comparing the economic wealth of those who did not migrate through the Indentureship system with those who migrated and remained in the then colonies and now "independent" countries.

However, even though a majority of people of Indian origin (PIOs) are literate and have visible signs of economic wealth, they do not have any economic or political **power** in the now "independent" colonies where they are domiciled. We can cite Fiji, Guyana, Trinidad & Tobago, Suriname, Mauritius, South Africa, England, USA and Canada as indisputable examples. In comparison one is compelled to acknowledge the political power people of African origin possess in the now "independent" colonies. Take for example the entire Caribbean region and the USA: even though, as in

Trinidad & Tobago and Guyana specifically, people of African origin are not the statistical majority, nor do they, as a group, possess over-riding economic wealth, they do sit at the political dinner table and formulate and pass laws with which the entire country is to be governed.

Apparently PIOs do not wish to participate in, contribute to, or support social, civil or political progress. They would rather fuel the two wheels of the unstable two-wheel vehicle they proudly ride – the economic wheel and the "religious" wheel while other groups are safer and more stable in a their four-wheel vehicles – the political wheel, the political-religious wheel, the political-economic wheel, and the political-cultural wheel.

I guess that the PIOs understanding of the realities of the world is seriously handicapped. Or, perhaps, the British did a greater and better number on them and, as such, they are comfortable to continue as the laboring class just as their fore-parents, even though Identureship has been abolished one century ago. Maybe PIOs have self-contracted themselves and established a covenant with their god(s) to remain as indentured laborers. Evidently, this is their choice.

There are the few PIO "scholars" who write and make speeches here and there for their personal ego boosts and parade as leaders. Whom have they led? From where to where have they led whom when their writings and body politic continue to present themselves as victims of the Identureship system and/or being oppressed by the ruling political party/elite.

One hundred years after the said British abolished the Identureship system that was designed by the British to supply labor to their colonies, PIOs, who have been deemed the greatest success as able-bodied laborers in/on the estates, still today remain the greatest success as laborers in the countries in which they reside. For them Time has stood still. Their "learned" pandits, in their statue-bedecked mandirs, continue to focus their minds back to some 5000 years ago and keep them permanently there.

"Indians Arrival Day" is celebrated in many Caribbean countries, including Guyana. In Grenada this day is celebrated as a public holiday in conjunction with Labor Day.

In Guyana a gala event was organized in May 2017 to celebrate the one hundredth anniversary of the abolition of the British designed "Identureship System." The Afro-Guyanese President, David A. Granger attended the function paying tribute to the contributions of Indo-Guyanese to Guyana.

Photos of celebration in Guyana: Govt. of Guyana release.

Above: Cross section of Guyanese in attendance at the 100 Anniversary Celebration in Guyana. Below: Indo-Guyanese dancers performing to celebrate and mark the event.

<u>Above:</u> Drumming art form retained by Indo-Guyanese and displayed at the 100th Anniversary function in Guyana.

In Trinidad & Tobago major Indo-T&T Organizations such as the Maha Sabha, the Indian Cultural Council and the Indian Diaspora Council, among others, collaborated in a unified event to mark and celebrate the

100th Anniversary of the abolition of Identureship in March 2017. The highlight of the function was the laying of a commemorative plaque in T&T.

<u>Above</u> The commemorative Plaque in T&T by IDC Member, Darrel.

"FOR FEELINGS": Essay #14

They did not know what to do with the small group of teenagers. According to them these teenagers were not only useless they were hopeless. Why bother with them? Why care about them? They were drug abusers.

As the Program Coordinator and Senior Counselor I decided to accept them in the Program and to personally instruct them.

The first day we encountered each other in the classroom, my topic for discussion was, "Why people take drugs?" We were to discuss this topic openly and freely, without any projection to blame any one; we were to deal with the topic dispassionately and impersonally.

I am not sure I know why "my" students "opened up" to me. We can speculate but it is not necessary. They soon opened up to me and began speaking freely about why they thought people take drugs. I allowed and encouraged them to verbally express themselves without being judgmental or condescending and suggested that they make personal notes since they were required to write an essay on the said topic. The discussion was adjourned to the next day's lesson so that all who wanted to say their piece had an opportunity to do so.

By the third day we came to the conclusion that people take drugs "to feel good." I then asked "my" students that, "if you want to 'feel good,' why not do something "good" for yourself? If you do something "good" for yourself, you will feel "good." You do not have to take drugs to feel "good." I asked them to wash the dishes in the sink when they went home that day.

The next day we followed up on what I asked them to do. Even though I expected them to do as I asked, I was pleasantly surprised to learn that all of them did as I asked. I asked them how they felt after they washed the dishes. They all said that they "felt good." I then asked them to vacuum the carpet in the living room. Again they did. And again I asked them how they felt after they finished vacuuming the carpet. They said that they felt "good."

I concluded that people do things to "feel good," among other reasons. Why do we have sex if not to "feel good?" Obviously, we do not have sex to "feel bad." There are some who have sex solely to procreate. Anyway, no need to speculate here.

I have heard many a persons say that she/he **feels** that the charged person is guilty. Can one feel that another is guilty? Must one convict another on the basis her/his feelings or on the established facts? But then, who has the mental faculties to differentiate what is fact from what is fiction and from what are merely one's feelings. The majority of folks acts upon, and acts out, their feelings condemning innocent people. Acting upon one's feelings of fear can lead to murder. And then there is the "thrill of the kill," especially in hunting and in war.

How often do we not see a remorseful individual, on the road to repenting and recovering, regret and lament her/his actions, which actions she/he took on the basis of her/his feelings? Are our feelings to be trusted as a basis for action?

The individual takes a few extra alcoholic drinks, of course, because of how the alcohol makes her/him feel. She/he then attempts to drive/operate a motor vehicle to get home. How often does she/he not get home, but ends up killing some one and landing herself/himself in the hospital with very serious injuries?

The eldest son would come home and sit with his mother and hug her and kiss her and make her laugh. It is likely that this behavior of her eldest son made her "feel good." The last son would be cooking in the kitchen while mom and brother were entertaining themselves in the living room. Later the last son would serve dinner to his mom and, of course, his eldest brother. Which of the two sons, do you think, the mother considered to be the good son?

When asked which of the two sons should inherit the family residence, which one do you think she insisted should get it? She insisted the eldest son, the one that made her laugh and "feel good," of course.

So many millions of individuals are looking for a "match!" So, the parents of the young woman want her to get married to a financially stable fellow. Of course, she cannot not see the wisdom of the basis of their choice. Or, maybe she just wants to rebel against her parents, now that she is an adult. For, after all, what do her parents know? And, it is her life; only she must have a say in what happens in her life. So she chooses the fellow she loves – the one who makes her feel a particular way; the one who can give her the best sex; the one with whom she can have fun and more fun. She marries him and, about two years later, they are divorced, leaving her with the responsibility of two children! All for feelings!

Counseling some of "my" students about coming to class late, I asked them why they are late. All of them stated that did not want to be late and that they did not like to be late. "Why are you usually late, then?" I asked them. They did not have a satisfactory answer, satisfactory to themselves. They were unhappy with themselves when they were late, which was often. We had to correct this unwanted behavior.

I informed them that they were late, even though they did not want to be late, because they were posing the wrong question to themselves when they were about to get out of bed.

I told them that they were asking themselves about their feelings; they were asking themselves how they were feeling. I pointed out to them that, instead of asking themselves how they were feeling, they should ask themselves what they had to do that day. "When it is cold outside and you have your sex partner lying next to you, how would you feel? Would you feel to get out of bed? Of course not! If, however, you were to ask yourself 'what do I have to do today?' you will quickly yank yourself out of bed to get to what you have to do. Try it and let's see how it works for you."

It worked for them. Their lateness to class was corrected and they completed the academic program.

When I listen to the so-called "news" by the so-called "main stream" media, they talk in what they call "sound-bytes." They then proceed to give their opinions, which, as they say, is the way they **feel**. They **feel** that Hilary Clinton should win. They **feel** that the Russians interfered in the national election of 1916, which resulted in Donald J. Trump winning. There are no facts or evidence. There isn't even a statement as what the Russians actually did. They inform the public about how they **feel**. Are the **feelings** of someone news? What is news? Who decides what news is?

Thankfully, Donald J. Trump has the guts to call what the so-called "main stream" media labels "news" fake-news. Most what is broadcasted by the "main-stream" media is fake news because the talking heads constantly give their opinions. In addition to their opinions they call upon two or three of their friends from the Washington Post and the New York Times to give their **feelings** and opinions. Opinions and opinions and more opinions – fake news!

Thankfully, there is "social media." Folks do not have to

depend on "main stream" media for "news" or to be informed as to what happened when or to have to hear the opinions and **feelings** of four to six like-minded "journalists" as "news."

"THE GUYANA SITUATION" Essay #15

They write. The "brilliant scholars" write. They write about being discriminated. They write about their being discriminated in Guyana. But, according to these "brilliant scholars," the Guyana situation is getting worse and worse. This, of course, begs the question, "why do they write?" What is the specific purpose of their writings? What changes are taking place because of their writing?

Why this present interest by Indo-Guyanese in the political and economic conditions in Guyana as is exemplified by the proliferation of their numerous articles in small uninfluencial newspapers, the best use of which is to wrap fish?

They couch and cloak their ignorance and prejudices under headings of "lack of democracy," "workers sufferance," "crime and corruption," and the like. They write. Perhaps they write just because they can write, or just to fill column-inches in the papers owned by their friends. Whatever the reason, they write.

Like Jagan, who said that, "if there is free and fair election, the PPP will win," but who could NOT ever achieve this desirable prerequisite for Democracy in his lifetime, these "brilliant scholars" continue to write about the current "lack of democracy" in Guyana but they will never be able to correct the situation. What effect do their writings have, and on whom?

Guyanese, especially Indo-Guyanese, are the most ungrateful and misdirected group of people. And, as such, one must ask the question, why spend one's own resources of time, money and knowledge so that they can benefit? What makes them deserving of intervention by expatriates and the friends of expatriates? When they prospered, as is noticeable, under the PPP government, did they make any contribution of time, money, or knowledge to international organizations or individuals who spent the best part of their lives and resources fighting in the international arena for the restoration of Democracy in Guyana? The answer is" No!" Did the PPP government or any of its members make a donation to the Carter Center, the said Center that declared that the PPP won over the Voice of America in 1992? "No!" If this is not the best example of ungratefulness, what else is?

Now Guyanese are crying "May Day!" "May Day!" yet again. They do not deserve it. If however, democracy were to be again restored, who would be the beneficiary, which political party? The answer is the PPP. This is the same PPP that benefited in 1992. As the General Secretary of the World Union of Democracy, USA, nominated by Ravi Dev, and unanimously elected, at a meeting in Jim Bacchus' building on Liberty Ave in Richmond Hill, NYC and in a private meeting with the now deceased Congressman Steven Solars of Brooklyn, NY, I was asked this question: "Roop, when we get free and fair election in Guyana, wouldn't that fellow Jagan and his party win? But Jagan is a Communist! Why bother, Roop?" There is the irony: a Communist is asking Capitalists to restore Democracy in Guyana so that he, the Communist would win in the national election.

Why didn't the PPP "change the constitution?" while they were in the majority in the Guyanese Parliament? They didn't because they, like Burnham and his PNC, were the beneficiaries of a constitution designed to give much sweetness to the "ruling" political party – paramountcy to the PNC and PPP parties, why change anything?

Why didn't President Dr. Jagan, or President Mrs. Jagan, or Jagan's surrogate, President Jagdeo did what is necessary to improve the working and union conditions of the sugar workers? After almost half a century of "independence" the sugar workers are no better off than when Booker/Tate and Lyle were the major owners of the sugar industry. What a shame! What is the benefit of "independence?" Clearly the sugar workers have NOT benefited.

The fact of the matter is sugar is no longer "king." People all over the world are reducing their intake of sugar. There is a reduction in the demand for edible sugar. Also, France is a major producer of sugar from sugar beets. Why should European countries buy sugar from Guyana when an EU member country is producing sugar to meet their reduced demands? Why doesn't Russia buy Guyana's sugar since the PPP claims to be a Communists comrade? If there were a quota system developed with Russia during the PPP regime (as Communist comrades), there would now be no need to lay off sugar workers.

Further, when, in 1992, ex-president Carter announced that the PPP won the election when only 42% of the ballots were counted and immediately left Guyana, did the PPP complain about the "lack of democracy?" Of course not! They celebrated and reaped all the benefits as if they had worked for them. Now the same ex-president Carter declared the PNC the winner and immediately left the country. The PPP and its Indo-Guyanese surrogates are complaining about "lack of democracy." I wonder, to whom are they complaining? Why should anyone answer their SOS call yet again?

<u>Expect Volume 2</u>

*Aurora Spring is the penname of the writer. He has done extensive work to restore Democracy in Guyana. Guyana was able to realize "free and fair" elections in 1992 and a 28-year dictatorship was **peacefully** removed. The writer was the founding member of the World Union of Guyanese for Democracy, USA and was elected its General Secretary. In his work for the cause of Democracy he wrote to every member of the US Congress, typing with one finger on a small portable typewriter. Unfortunately, as a result of the country realizing "free and fair" elections with assistance from the Carter Center, a communist party leader, who was unable to accomplish this feat for his lifetime, benefited from the conscientious work of the writer, in particular. To bring the cause of the lack of Democracy in Guyana and the dictatorial rule of its then "president for life" to the attention of the UN, the writer organized a 7-day fast in the Dag Hammarskjold plaza in NYC and fasted there for 7 days.*

To his credit the writer has worked continuously and tirelessly for over three decades to create and establish the Indo-Caribbean Identity in the New York City's socio-cultural environment. With his consultation, management and leadership, the first Indo-Caribbean was elected to New York State Assembly.

As the General Secretary of the Indo-Caribbean Council, (ICC-NY) an organization he co-founded with his boyhood friend, the writer is always ready to represent the interest of Indo-Caribbeans. In executing the Mission of the ICC-NY, the Council has recognized many deserving Caribbeans, including the one-time Prime Minister of T&T, and the Prime Minister of Grenada & Grenadines. In fact, when women were being kidnaped and ransomed in T&T, he organized "The Trinidad & Tobago Focus Group" and led a delegation to T&T to address and resolve the then political impasse in T&T. As the General Secretary of the ICC-NY he convened the first civic function in the Indo-Caribbean Community to commemorate the achievements of the Civil Rights Movement (USA), which was led by Dr. Martin Luther King, Jr. who was influenced by the greatest, Mahatma Gandhi of India.

He was instrumental in formalizing the Indo-Caribbean Federation of NA, which is still functioning, by writing its By-Laws and holding the Organization's first election. He was elected its first General Secretary. He helped found and wrote the By-Laws of many NGOs operating in Queens County, New York.

When New York State decided to recognize the Guyanese Community for their contributions to the economy of the state of New York, the writer was invited, with two others, to receive the Proclamation and Resolution that marked this historic event. With his associate and colleague the writer co-founded the first school for professional development in Queens, NY, which school, with his continuous contribution, continues to exist (while others have been closed) and certify thousands in the real estate industry.

Quotes from the writer: *"Academic pursuits should not prevent you from living socially fruitful lives."*
"An individual without culture is naught, but like a dry leaf, to be blown which ever way the wind chooses."
"Not every human form houses a human being." "Things do not just happen; people make things happen"